COMPUTERS AT LARGE

Also by Charles J. Sippl

Computer Dictionary and Handbook
Microcomputer Dictionary and Guide
Calculator Users Guide and Dictionary
Data Communications Dictionary
Microcomputer Handbook

Charles J. Sippl & Robert Bullen

Computers At Large

The Bobbs-Merrill Company, Inc.
Indianapolis/New York

Published by the Bobbs-Merrill Company, Inc.
Indianapolis New York

Designed by Winston Potter
Manufactured in the United States of America

First printing

Library of Congress Cataloging in Publication Data

Sippl, Charles J
Computers at large.

1. Computers and civilization. I. Bullen,
Robert, joint author. II. Title.
QA76.9.C66S56 301.24'3 73-22675
ISBN 0-672-51907-0

Contents

COMPUTERS AT LARGE

chapter 00001

The Intellectual Impact of Man's Thinking Machine

In these first days of the last quarter-century of the millennium, people have come to realize that the friendly neighborhood computer—or the one or network of them off at the Internal Revenue Service and the Federal Bureau of Investigation—is taking over more than just recordkeeping.

Suddenly they find that they themselves have become part of the network. And the network has become The Network, a means for the federal government to tie together the various hitherto independent files of government and private agencies. By means of a new technology, IMP (an acronym, fittingly devilish if too diminutive, for "interface message processor"), the "language problem" that had been keeping computer models and systems apart has been overcome. IMP instantaneously translates the languages of other machines into one that fits any particular system. This means that, despite past congressional opposition to the establishment of a formal network (at one time called FEDNET), the bureaus and branches of government, principally the White House, the CIA, the FBI, the IRS and the Department of Defense, have been able to bring together facts about every American at any time they are needed, in any so-called emergency. So reported Ford Rowan on NBC Nightly News in June 1975. Through Social Security, Selective Service, the state motor-vehicle bureaus, the interlocking tax structures, the multitudinous government service and welfare programs, political contributions and activities, not to mention the law enforcement and internal security agencies, so many things every citizen does are on record. The problem is, those records aren't safe. They can be accessed (computerese for looked up, added to, duplicated, transferred), tampered with, even sold, by anyone with authorization to obtain any of the files. Links can be set up at will between computers and broken apart at will when they've served their purpose, with no trace left of whatever transfer of records has taken place. It's a complicated (yet ultimately simple) developing story that changes with every morning's Today show.

Suddenly, too, something else becomes obvious, perhaps even more serious: computers and computer-driven machines are becoming cheaper than people for many jobs. They're more productive, and productivity is what computers and an industrial society are all about. Once expensive and complex, computers—not simple calculators—are cheap, easy to use, easy to carry about, easy to plug in and plug out, commonplace.

The question remains, however, are these machines monsters—or the sires or creatures of monsters, as hair-raising sci-fi has been predicting—or are they beneficent and controllable? Better, are the people who put them to work beneficent and controllable?

There are few simple answers to these and many other questions about computers. And common sense may not always be the best guide in a realm where x^2 is equal to x. However, the principal benefit from a free-wheeling approach to the subject such as this book offers is to get everything (well, almost everything) out on the line. Neat presentations elsewhere—in books, on television and in the press—are often overly simple or too couched in trade and technical terms. They beg many questions, for discussions of computer-related matters pose many chicken-and-egg enigmas: computer information systems invade privacy, but protection of privacy is a noncomputer, legal, political concern; computer-aided automation by its nature has to do people out of work, yet it's noncomputer social awareness that's going to correct the evils of technological dislocation.

What concept comes first? What does this or that relate to? These are typical of the puzzles that have to trouble anyone who finds himself anywhere beneath the surface of the computer story. Because of the complexity of the subject, there will be repetitions in the book. There have to be. There will be stretches of math and technology, not as replacements of textbooks or equipment manuals, but to at least confront the important intellectual base the great structure rests on. The math and technology crop up in the coverage of privacy, and vice versa. Privacy intrudes on the subject of disemployment, and vice versa.

Computers think. Or, if they don't, what they accomplish equals thought, and, by the performance of intellectual functions in immeasurable blinks of time, they extend human thought. They make possible mathematical, statistical and analytical feats that man without the computer would not dare to propose, let alone undertake. Computers have proved theorems in plane geometry; played and won at chess and checkers; composed, arranged and played music; created interesting graphic patterns; and even simulated human speech—one, at Bell Laboratories, read a story—

> the north wind and the sun were arguing one day, when a traveler came along, wrapped in a warm coat . . .

—though pleading, like a good puppet, that it understood

not a word of what it recited. Others solve problems in calculus, and indeed have proved crucial in the opening up of whole new systems of mathematics.

With all their awe-inspiring capabilities, computers create a new set of problems. A man with a balanced checkbook is notified that he has a bad credit rating; but his bills are paid. Well, try to get to the source of the bad rating. Your lighting bill is wrong; try to correct it. An engineer is laid off, not for incompetence but because his name has turned up on a computerized list of people attending a local protest rally. A high school girl gets her name into the files of the FBI for having written a letter to a Trotskyite party office as part of her schoolwork. Without a computer, dealing only with the physical files of a bureaucracy—hard data—the victim could have some trouble correcting the damage, but with favorable court rulings or a cooperative agency, he or she could gain access to, and correct or remove, the actual file. When dealing with a computer, the source of the damage is remote. By its nature, the file of the computer can never assuredly be corrected by any of the means at the outsider's disposal. In a computer file there is no original—something that members of Congress and civil-rights lawyers are coming gradually to realize. Promises of removal can be carried out only by the programmer, the person at the input terminal. And even when this is done, who's to say which other node in a network of computers might have a duplicate of what you're after?

Computers store, manipulate, and need never forget vast amounts of detailed information. Once the computer begins to process information, events move inexorably forward, justly or unjustly, humanely or not. Recent legislation offers us some protection from the remoteness and complexity of the process. However, allegations of abuses can bring about costly litigation. Granted redress or not, with the computer our actions can go into records and remain, subject to all kinds of uncontrolled cross-referencing and transferring. Our pasts remain for others to discover and evaluate for years to come. A statute of limitations seems not to apply, nor do ordinary rules of evidence. Within a few years of 1984 (George Orwell's whammy on the future and the future machine), the "tracks" we leave enmesh us in a great system of control. It's irritating, and not a little scary.

At the core of the paranoia and justified concern is the increasing accessibility of computers to our governments, industries and social institutions. A favorite bromide is that a computer is only as bad, or good, as the people who feed and use it. But with the proliferation of computers, the problem of checking and controlling the keepers, the feeders and users becomes a chief matter for each of us to be informed about. Don't ask for whom the tape whirs; it whirs for thee.

Zero growth is what the computers might prescribe for an overpopulated earth, but not for themselves. Their numbers multiply. Their use becomes cheaper because of the number of functions each is able to perform (the economy of scale), and because of miniaturization, making possible sophisticated "machines" that fit into the palm of your hand and sell, in 1975, for less than a thousand dollars. There are standard computers, minicomputers and microcomputers. They all perform any number of tasks with precision, speed and versatility unmatched by humans. The jobs they do would be impractical or impossible for anything but another computer to duplicate. They can be built to detect and correct errors in their own performance and to indicate which of their components is producing the error. They can automatically disconnect faulty parts and connect built-in spares. They can make decisions.

A computer is a logic machine, a decision-making apparatus. Its electrical structure, a microscopic pinball machine within the panel or case you see, is what does the work of computing. The "scoring" results from changes and exchanges of electrons. Within the terms of the code being used, these changing states mean things like "yes" or "no," "full" or "empty," "go" or "no go," "more" or "less," "true" or "false," "if this then that but not the other unless its capital is on a freshwater lake" (or some other such extravagantly discrete function or property). On the basis of instructions, criteria, "judgments" programmed into the machine, the electrical pulse and the magnetic state of each unit or cell cause the computer to "stop to think" and "make up its mind" about what to do every speed-of-light step of the way.

Computers can remember and search their memories for appropriate data that have been either programmed in with the instructions, or matched, acquired or "adapted" in the process of manipulating new data. So they can learn from experience, probabilities and new discoveries from within themselves, or from other computers which they are triggered, by their programs, to access and probe. They receive information in more codes and sensory modes than man can, and at rates millions of times faster. Six times eight is forty-eight, as any second-grader will tell you in an instant. How fast is an instant? A computer receives, perceives, stores and retrieves data in microseconds (millionths of a second); processes the data in nanoseconds (billionths); and some can work in picoseconds (trillionths). A typical large computer will do 20 million additions a second.

Computers can replace people in the areas of data processing, simulation and automation. They are untiring, more accurate, faster, more productive. The job computers do in data processing is well known—keeping track of insurance records and making calculations, updating the phonebook, payrolls, any number of massive tasks. The Social Security system, for instance, maintained fifty-two computer systems at its Baltimore facility in 1972, and from there made out and mailed 27 million checks a month.

Computers are also assigned tasks of analysis that involve so many factors—fixed, variable or random—that no man or team of men could conceive of them (let alone take them on). Here they are made to act as models or simulations of real processes, in order to bring problems to the point of decision, leaving man the last word. (It's to be hoped!) Connected to sensors, and governing mechanisms in robots, computers do repetitive, but alterable, mechanical tasks.

Time is money. Technological advances, miniaturization of components, and automated manufacture have brought down the costs of computers, made them more available; and even the expensive machines and systems are more powerful, capable of many more times their previous operations. There's a law in the trade, Grosch's law, which states that the processing power of a computer increases proportionately with the square of the cost. In other words, a $2 million system does four times the work of a $1 million system. As things have developed, Grosch's ratio itself has expanded. It's more like the cost to the power of 2.5 in scientific computing, and to the cube (or third power) in business—to double the cost gives five times the processing, or six, as the case may be. Could anyone ever have bought a car on any such rule of thumb?

Everyone out to get his smarts

Nineteen seventy-four was the year of a lot of things—Richard Nixon's resignation, mainly; but it was also the year, in the face of inflation, in which low-cost pocket calculators burst into stores and newspaper ads. What's Macy's doing selling "business machines"? But these were not, by a far cry, office equipment. Everyone who was anyone, on expense account or not, had to have a calculator to call his own at the cheapest price and with the most functions possible, even if he couldn't work them all. For thirty dollars and even less, in 1974, you were able to buy and hold in your hand a battery-driven machine that did what desk models twenty times the price and size had done two years before. And for the price of the old desk model ($600 or so) you were now able to get a hand calculator that not only added, subtracted, multiplied and divided (what the thirty-dollar models did), but also did trigonometry, logarithms, square roots, raising to a power, statistics of all sorts, and many special business and financial calculations as well. What was more, such a near-computer allowed you to program (enter into the machine your algorithm, or recipe, for the work to be done) and to run standard programs. At a list price of less than fifty dollars, a set of standard programs—say the medical pack—would contain twenty-odd magnetic cards for insertion into the calculator. The cards carried programs for long, involved operations such as setting up and calibrating a breathing apparatus and interpreting lung-function test results.

A step beyond the calculators in power and price, using the same miniature circuits and switches but tuned to a higher degree of response and adaptability, are the microcomputers. Also given names like "naked minis" and "microprocessors," such units serve as the eyes, ears, brains and hands of automatic tellers, traffic-light controllers, and so on. Selling in quantity (orders of 1,000, 5,000, and 10,000) for as little as twenty-five dollars apiece, microprocessors go into the products of original equipment manufacturers (OEMs for short), the makers of the ultimate marketed product—a sewing machine, for instance, or, in the case of computers, a terminal. As small as they are, ⅛ inch square in some cases, microprocessors compute and process; they determine and bring about courses of action; they appear as intelligent (that is, interactive) communicators to the hundreds of interface systems—people and machines—that deal with them. They're smart.

Smart terminals, visual input and output equipment, have moved into everyday life. They consist mainly of a TV screen (called a CRT, for cathode-ray tube) and a typewriter keyboard. As point-of-sale terminals they are in supermarkets and department stores; they are automated tellers in banks and even act as branches for banks in busy public places; they handle reservations, billing, scheduling, dispatching in hotels, offices, hospitals, utilities, schools, public services like police, fire and sanitation—all with little or no clerical supervision.

Electronics, a trade magazine, describes the use of a microprocessor in eyeglass frames which organizes images and transmits them to electrodes implanted in the brain, so providing some modicum of sight to the blind.

Pleading its own case in the Justice Department's antitrust action against it, IBM capsulizes the reverse economics of the computer business:

> . . . costs have declined as rapidly as performance has improved. Costs relative to effective computing speeds have decreased by a factor of 80 since the first processors. The cost of tape drive units relative to performance has decreased by 150 times. The cost of disk storage capacity has decreased by 36 times. The overall cost of doing 100,000 multiplications has declined from $1.26 in 1952 to $.26 in 1958, to $.12 in 1964, to $.05 in 1970, and to $.01 in 1974, and all of these decreases in cost have been accomplished during a period of continuing inflation which has increased the cost of other products.

When a bargain's not a bargain

So with a lively, aggressive market keeping down prices on computers of any size or complexity, or else with higher prices paying for more power exponentially, smart machines and intelligent systems become commonplace. And for all the good they obviously promise and do, it's important to once more look critically at the potential dangers inherent in this proliferation.

Before proceeding further, it's imperative that we have a clear idea of which problems relate to computers and which do not. In our desire to apportion blame for society's ills, are we letting computers stand for technology itself? Are we letting technology stand for political and social ineptitude, shortsightedness and cowardice? Computers and technology do displace people from their jobs—both white- and blue-collar. It's absurd, however, to contend that computers alone are responsible. A society that allows the computer-displaced worker—the "disemployed," we'll call him or her to distinguish from those unemployed for all the classic reasons—to just shift for himself with whatever benefits he has accrued, union or otherwise—that society, itself, is the culprit. Expanding use and dependence on computers in such a society merely increases the risks of depersonalization, dehumanization, treating people as things, "bits" or "bytes" in our programs.

Which came first, Nazi programming of a citizenry of goosestepping "good" Germans or the computer? Joseph Goebbels needed no IBM model 370 to work his or Hitler's way with the Third Reich. It's possible, however, that his efforts "invented" the computer in the aspects that so frighten us now. It's possible too that George Orwell's *1984* without a 370 was utopian and will prove naively out-of-date as we approach his doomsyear. (Winston Smith's speakwrite in the Ministry of Truth, incidentally, was hardly a computer, but a clanking, greasy paper sorter and shredder.) The drift here is that maybe our thinking, given a new force by the computer, is more the problem than is the computer itself.

Our thinking we can do for ourselves; the thinking the computers do for us would seem to have to be made to fit our powers of assimilation. We're not all being forced through unyielding tubes. Computers cannot be made into white knights conjured up to save us from every peril, nor into dragons that stand in the way of virtue.

Alvin Toffler's *Future Shock* and Marshall McLuhan's *Understanding Media*, popular manifestos of the "New Consciousness," are, for all their merit, shot through with some pretty fancy doublethink: technology is the ongoing force, the argument goes, and the dislocations of technology are results only of man's lack of nerve, rearview-mirror piloting. Well, it's more than that. Why, for instance—apart from plain evidence of abusive authority—is there so much concern in the mid-1970s with spying? Privacy and human rights have always been a concern; the Faustian potentialities of electronic data processing tend only to emphasize the dangers of interlocking systems of surveillance. Man's very right to the pursuit of happiness, if not life and liberty, is plainly on the line as computer-sensitized automation takes over more and more jobs (McLuhan doesn't like the word *job*), more and more industrial and service functions, and threatens obsolescence to whole industries and professions. Worries about the multiplying electronic presence surface like worms after a rain. Yet, worry, which is awareness without insight, is woefully inadequate. Instead, above all else, we must be concerned with information about computers, and information is hard to come by.

"Information" there is, but useful, objective information is elusive. The very structure and function of the machines have roots deep in the soil of symbolic logic and advanced mathematics, tough hoeing for the layman. There is no one computer industry. The firms and organizations, the professional and lay people that furnish the thinking and technology, and design, make and modify the systems as well as (now only tentatively) police them, are as various as the whole of industrial society itself. Everyone, it seems, is into computers. However, there is a lag and confusion in the publishing of information, caused by the jealous guarding of trade secrets and the exclusivity and competition among the manufacturers and users. Despite uncertainty about what computers can and can't do, the commitment to them grows steadily—from the smallest shop making specialized components, to the nursery school providing calculators for children, all the way up to the Department of Defense, constructing theoretical models for automated battlefields.

Computers are slaves; some like to call them idiots: they do only what their masters and keepers—men as well as other machines—tell them to do. They must always be programmed. Perhaps. Yet the trend, carefully explored in Rein Turn's *Computers in the 1980s*, is for hardware, which is the processing unit and its "peripherals," as they're called (input/output and storage devices), to take over more of the nonmachine (software) functions. Microprocessors now contain fixed instructions, or firmware, a third main division of computer anatomy. With circuitry arranged to handle functions heretofore left to software, firmware allows the nonprofessional to take his place at the controls and the machine to do more of the work unattended. The operator's work is lightened to the extent that firmware provides the machine with routines that the operator himself would otherwise have to provide. A limp analogy, but helpful, might be the piano roll for difficult passages that would be common to a number of pieces and that the "artist" could access at will or (more in keeping with talk of firmware) that the instrument itself would insert or interpose at appropriate intervals.

There are unlimited possibilities for the development of new firmware and programs, new systems and new applications. The simplest programming devices—the magnetic slip-in cards for the advanced calculators, the $600 models—

are, in a sense, themselves machines. They, the plug-in microprocessors and cassettes, each perform unique tasks. They are interchangeable among the larger systems and are duplicable. They are bought and sold, rented and copied among manufacturers and users. While large software systems are worth upward of $100,000, because they are unique and represent a great amount of work, they are, according to a ruling by the Supreme Court in 1972, not patentable.

Huge banks of valuable programs are available for nominal fees; you simply describe your problem and order a program to match it. Software houses specialize in cataloging, abstracting and indexing programs. They act as middlemen and rent, trade or sell from their files programs that have been developed by every type of user, from student to atomic physicist. Practically every major computer manufacturer has its own user group which maintains a library of member-developed programs that are swapped back and forth. General Electric's Mark III Information Services is the largest of several great computer-network services. GE connects more than 100 computers throughout the world. Access to them is by way of local telephone in 400-odd cities, in the United States, Canada, Western Europe, Japan and Australia. Subscribers can list and give abstracts of their own programs as an offer to sell or rent, or they can inquire about programs available to them from the service library. GE will transmit the program and bill for it in seconds. Adaptation or translation of a program to work with supposedly noncompatible machines is no problem. Here again, microprocessors do a job: they can serve as emulators (IMPs) to enable the subscriber's computer to accept "foreign" programs and machine languages.

The GE service introduced telephone information processing (TIP) in 1975. TIP uses Votrax, a digital voice synthesizer, not unlike the Bell Lab experiments, which converts TouchTone signals into human speech—a truly remarkable breakthrough that we're sure to hear much more about. The simple effect of TIP on the service Mark III supplies is to synthesize quick verbal responses (in plain, unaccented English) to questions put to the computers—no need for elaborate terminals, keyboards and printers.

Seemingly without letup the computer feeds, and feeds upon, technology. To question the public's readiness is futile, as futile as would be an order to halt or reverse the process. Ready or not, man is being moved by instantaneous information into a new age. He is being forced to abandon old ways and attitudes about himself. In McLuhan's words, ". . . Western man, were he determined to cling to the fragmented and individualist ways that he has derived from the printed word in particular, would be well advised to scrap all his electric technology since the telegraph." Granted this is not the choice, man can't at the same time ignore the immediate effects. Social changes need not be glacial or explosive, sweeping or blowing away so much of what we know and believe. Human values can matter and not be buried in the interests of progress or inevitability. Men do lose jobs and livelihoods because of automation—dignity and purpose, too. It's not enough to promise the dislocated, the disemployed, that all will come out enriched and new in the end. The costs of automation can be made part of any program that displaces men and women from jobs. This is feedback that no complete servoloop can do without. Automation and data processing are adopted by public and private institutions to save money and increase efficiency. In systems-biz parlance, they are cost-effective. Till the human costs are put into the equation, however, the bottom line will be just numbers, and not add up to what society will eventually have to pay to straighten out the inequities and dislocations.

To repeat, man's *use* of the computer is what is subject

to judgment and control. The executives of Equity Funding Corporation of America entered 56,000 fabricated insurance policies into their IBM system and thereby defrauded the reinsurance companies they dealt with of $20 million. The face value of the phony policies was over $2 billion. The fraud could not have been attempted without the computer, but eighteen people have been convicted of the crime. The computer's complicity is nowhere in consideration. As an instrument, the computer can magnify the extent of manipulation and make detection nearly impossible. (Detection is often accidental.)

(Statements about the percentage of computer crimes that go undetected are rhetorical exaggerations. Typically the figure given is 85 percent. Eighty-five percent of what? How can anyone know what 100 percent represents if eighty-five out of a hundred remain undetected? Separating computer fraud as a category from garden-variety—salad oil—fraud is not easy, though the separation has to be attempted if the appropriate controls are to be devised.)

You can program computers for all sorts and levels of integrity and security, and bad or shoddy programming can itself invite tampering, but we can't lose sight of man as the agent of whatever the abuse: fraud, invasion of privacy, disemployment without equitable resettlement of the displaced—the Plains Indians of the electric age.

Computers cannot take the blame for man, nor likewise take the blame for technology as a whole. Peter Drucker writes:

> . . . in the past sixty years man's view of technology itself has changed. We no longer see it as concerned with *things* only; today it is a concern of man as well. As a result of this new perspective, we have come to realize that technology is not, as our grandparents believed, the magic wand that can make all human problems and limitations disappear. We now know that technological potential is, indeed, even greater than they thought. But we have also learned that technology, as a creature of man, is

as problematical, as ambivalent, and as capable of good or evil, as its creator.

As a force, technology and the industrial engine it stokes must of necessity treat man as an object. Switches and signals on railroads went wrong before computers controlled them, and people died in the wrecks the malfunctions caused. They stood around in stalled trains in snowstorms and were treated like and felt like cattle in the face of remote authority at work, or asleep, or gone wild. And to remove the analogy from the industrial context, aborigines, religious outsiders, the misfits of any sort wherever man has plied his aggression, have been used and decimated, numbered and numbed, swiftly as with the Jews in Nazi Europe, grindingly as with the blacks and Indians in the free New World. It doesn't do, as does Charles A. Reich in *Greening of America*, to glorify the gradualness of change in the preindustrial past in order to damn the devastating uprootings of technology. Technology disposes of man as an object, quantifies him; this is certain. If, however, man is to remain man and do something more than just reject or adapt, he'll do so with the computer, with technology. In order to talk back, to manage, to control, he'll want to know better the ground he stands on and the tools and weapons he has at hand. With the computer too, he'll strive to assert himself—to make part of the firmware, the stochastic unknown, his tastes, his nonrational certainties, which no projection or simulation dealing with the individual can long ignore.

At present, this human self-assertion has run into problems. Take an innocent procedural exposition of the man-machine interplay by Rein Turn:

> Executive and operating systems (EOS) are the central control for all software, and must maintain orderly control of the interfaces among application programs, peripheral devices, and personnel. The EOS schedules work, handles interrupts, processes interrupts, assesses priorities, schedules and controls I/O [input/output],

allocates core storage, and provides recovery capability in the event of errors or unusual conditions.

People (personnel!) have a place in this scheme, but it's hard to glimpse the humanity, hard to see what choices one might have when the man-to-man relationship has been changed into this kind of man-machine link. Here we find ourselves several times removed from the contract an employee makes with his employer. Man has put himself, in Turn's paradigm, into the machine's (the system's) program. It's not clear that choice has much play in this process.

The man-machine interaction is not about who presses what knob. It's about the extension of brain through the machine which the brain itself has created. It's a leap-frogging of intellect and intellect-tool that can well prove infinite. No one has the vaguest notion of where it will lead. Scientists talk about the (lower-case) systems they're familiar with in their specialties (biology, physics, whatever), and seldom about the System, the Cybernetic System, with man and his extensions in the cycle, or loop. Philosophers address the meaning of propositions and not the meaning of the universe; politicians, the tactics of power and not the strategy of government. There are likely to be higher orders of systems that we haven't begun to comprehend. For all the information needed to specify the smallest living organism, there's more specifying to be done on you and me. In us, evolution has reached—at least temporarily and so far as we know—a finite limit. The personal computer in the cerebrum of the brain is hemmed in by bone and is constrained by a limiting number of neurons and by the limiting need to process and propagate the nerve impulse. There might be merit to the notion that man is no more than part of an evolutionary design that includes his own extension—the machine.

Some scientists face squarely the dangers inherent in

atomic nuclear fission and fusion. Few, however, have confronted the progress of cybernetics, the science of systems control. Cybernetics is not simply about clanking robots. "Intelligent" computers, "smart" machines, are much more. They impart adaptive behavior to an otherwise stop-and-start mechanism, steering it through a changing environment.

In his epochal work, *Cybernetics, or Control and Communication in the Man and the Machine* (1948), Norbert Wiener adapted the word for the new science of control from the Greek word *kybernetes,* which means literally "steersman," the man at the helm. Both the Greeks (specifically, Plato and Xenophon) and the Romans (who turned the word into the Latin *gubernator*) likened the arts of piloting—boats, chariots—to the arts of governing men. Cicero, who had his turn at the tiller of state, said *gubernare me taedebat* (governing bored me). Would that more aspirants to the helm had access to a similarly blithe indifference to power. Long before Wiener, in 1836 André Ampère, wandering out of his native science into an exhausting classification of all learning, used *cybernetics* to mean, in politics, the "function of governing." Then too, the word *governor,* as a regulating device in machinery, had long been a commonplace term in engineering. Wiener's originality lay in expanding the idea of the device itself, the servomechanism (as the governor came to be called in the complex work that was being done during World War II on radar and aiming systems), to the science of self-governing processes as a whole. It's interesting, this etymological linking of politics, science, automation and computers in the root words *servo* (from the Latin for "slave" and relating to the French, and then English, "serf"), *governor,* and *cybernetics.*

It raises again the worry that seems to leech itself to the strayest thought on the subject: the dilemma of the smart machine—master or slave? To look into the work of Wiener at the dawn of computer science can be enlightening. The need during the war for rapidity and precision in anti-aircraft implacements, bomb sights and other weaponry, the need for adding controls to radar that men weren't able to provide, mothered the development of sophisticated servo-loops. The work brought together scientists of many disciplines: physicists for analysis of the tasks as physical problems; mathematicians and engineers. The mathematicians went into arduous calculations having to do with stability; they got into matrix analysis, the logic of quantification, and transformation theory—the building blocks of computer theory and of much of the study that goes on still in machine and systems design. The engineers did their thing in electronics and materials research. Biologists too were involved as it became clear that there was an analogy between the behavior of the new machines and that of living organisms. The balancing of feedback with input in the servoprocess looked awfully like the reflex response in man.

The machines of the past acted like nothing but muscle, or receiving-and-sending organs; the new electrical marvels, with information actually at work inside like so much fuel or raw material, became organs trafficking in thought—pseudobrains. Such a notion had to breed intellectual revolution, and, by way of pollution, simplistic sci-fi dreck. Within the reach of scientific teaming, so the predictions went, were superior beings capable of electronic reproduction. The social process, itself working on changes in information, could be treated as a cybernetic system. A bold thrust in logic might design a future for man kept in order by regulating and thinking machines.

The implications are serious. The companies and people in the field downplay the scary side: the machine can't work without man, they say; the computer's not a brain. Still, man can't work any longer without the computer (think of the Social Security system for an instant), and neurologists, with their talk of electrochemical switches and circuits, find their best model for the brain in the computer.

Still too, control of the machine by the animal, who becomes part of it in the transaction, implies the reverse: control of the animal by the machine, an element in the cybernetic program from the first. From the start it was suspected that the same laws govern both. A man-versus-machine contest has seemed inevitable, and many of the reactions to abuses and supposed abuses have been skirmishes in what could turn into a war.

Cybernetics has to contend that man would do better to look upon himself and the machine as aspects, components, of the same process. Both are based on principles relating to the responsive, adaptive behavior of complex systems. The point is not that the cybernetic loop turns men and machines into the same thing, but that it describes both as consonant systems which are related to some larger system. It's at once a humbling and ennobling conception—by no means necessarily humiliating or debasing if a sense of humor and proportion is kept. How much does man dare to try?

Appropriately, some answers, and further questions, also appropriately, came forth at a conference held in 1972 to honor the memory of John von Neumann and his work twenty-five years before on the design of EDVAC. (Von Neumann had died in 1957.) EDVAC (Electronic Discrete Variable Automatic Computer), pre-UNIVAC, was one of the early one-of-a-kind machines to come out of the War Department's research on ballistics. It was the first fully modern electronic computer, the first containing a stored memory. Von Neumann's genius had already (in the 1920s) advanced set-theory in mathematics, and (in the 1930s) formulated the theory of games—the maximization of gain in situations of conflict. Both theories relate intricately to the structure and function of computation and computers.

In the quarter century following EDVAC, several hundred thousand computers were manufactured and installed throughout the world. Their impact was very real to those scientists assembled to honor their pioneer, and all could agree that the impact would continue.

The computer is indispensible, they also agreed, and would remain obedient to man, though unanimity on the meaning of *obedient* was not always clear from the variety of things that were said. There were the familiar fears: the ability of computers to simulate thinking, the implied threat to the primacy of man. The scientist and the computer? midwife to inhuman control? partner in urgent enterprises? Plainly, with more computers outside than inside scientific endeavors—government and business being the heaviest users—the impact of science on the computer, the computer on science, had not been nor would be negligible. The questions would continue to nag.

"Hard" scientists—physicists, chemists and their sort—routinely apply the computer to problems that were once totally insurmountable. Solutions and answers fundamental to the origin and meaning of life itself result. "It may be that the computer is the only one who really understands the kind of mathematics being done today," is how one of those present at the conference put it. Complex phenomena in the physical universe, beyond the comprehension of man, reduce themselves to the mathematical and logical workings of electronic circuits and arrays. From this, mathematicians and engineers derive their belief: the computer understands.

In any case, the computer and the brain are analogous, and electronic processes have created a new way of thinking. Psychologists point to a new and pervasive state of mind. They see men and computers as two different species of an abstract, higher genus called "information processing systems (IPS)." Some will insist that this simulation of mental activity in the machine and the shaping of mentality by cybernetics do not make a brain of the computer. Nonetheless, the computer metaphor is with us. It revives or fortifies a mechanistic view of life that's hard to shake. Met any IPS lately?

For all the quarrels and differences about mentality, the use of information processing systems (whatever man's place in them) confronts us with massive complexities. Constant and deepening inquiries have disclosed great openings into undiscovered sources of knowledge. We get hints of unlimited mysteries just beyond our next run of data and program. Beyond trial and error, beyond "hard" thinking and elegant, elegantly simple insights, the next problem and insight have always been lurking. The computer, as in all that it does, speeds the process and brings order to the intricate.

To see without seeing

There's more to it, too, than speed and order. Experimentation and investigation of logical formulations have till now depended on observation. With the computer and its talent for handling skeins of instructions—instructions that translate the most involved formulas and equations man can devise—scientists can observe a phenomenon or event without its actually having to take place. This is so because the computer can simulate reality; it represents systems and objects by numbers; it stores the numbers and manipulates them. In a booklet, *Simulation: Modeling Reality*, IBM does an unbeatable job of describing the theory and process:

> Perhaps the best known kind of simulation is that involving physical models. One may want to learn how a new wing configuration will affect the performance of an airplane, but to build the plane might require the expenditure of several million dollars, the commitment of a company's production resources, and a considerable amount of time. Instead, a physical model can be made and its performance measured in a wind tunnel. The model incorporates only those features of the plane that are

significant to its aerodynamic performance. Other elements, such as the design of its landing gear, the resolution of its radar, and the arrangement of its seats, are ignored, for none bears directly upon its function as an airfoil. These other features could be simulated in other models aimed at discovering other aspects of the plane's performance. Thus, any system or object could be represented in principle by an unlimited number of models.

The tested model might be, and often is, only one of a long series, because the design changes indicated by one test require the construction and testing of another, modified model. This process could conceivably go on indefinitely, for however many designs are tested, there might still be another that would be better. But at some point, modification and testing cease; the design is frozen, and the manufacturer, having saved much time and expense, begins production.

And yet, by a further step of abstraction, the design and testing burden can be lightened still more. When the model was installed in the wind tunnel and tested, numbers represented all the significant aspects of the test—the length of the wing, its curvature, the ratio of its surface to that of the fuselage, the velocities of the wind, the stresses on the wing induced by "flight," and the path of the slipstream.

Since the significant features of the model's performance are represented in numbers, and the sought-for answers consist of numbers, it is entirely logical and, with the computer, feasible to dispense with the physical materials of the test—the model, the tunnel, the wind—and represent them by the numbers that characterize them. For just as the plane's action on the air . . . can be simulated in the wind tunnel by blowing air past the model, so, by a further abstraction, can the action of the air on the model be represented in the computer by numbers that describe the wind's velocity and direction interacting with others that describe the form of the physical model.

The numbers may, obviously, deal with systems other than airplanes. They may deal with such tangible systems as communication networks and inventories, or such intangible ones as war strategies or a nation's economy. Indeed, whenever the consequences of an action or event must be known before it occurs and the real system is not available for experiment (. . . trial and error), or when mathematical analytical methods are inadequate to deal with the complexity of a problem, recourse can be had to simulation.

That's modeling. Its usefulness to science is plain, as is the data processing capability of computers: to collect and process the immensities of data that come out of experiments in labs and field studies, to reduce and analyze them, make the computer an obvious boon to research. This is especially true in disciplines where statistics is a big part of the load—psychology, sociology, economics. Economists, using computers, study the "flow of wealth" the way physicists study the "flow of heat." In experiments in the "hard" sciences, complex equipment is started and stopped and procedures changed hundreds and thousands of times by computer and the data recorded at each point.

Artificial intelligence, or genuine

So, pseudobrain or part of an IPS, analog of the brain or extension of brain and nervous system, the computer's "pretensions" to intellect are of major concern. The subject won't go away. Artificial intelligence has become the goal of much diverse research. It's not easy to define artificial intelligence; it seems to take on whatever meaning a particular study group puts to it. There are those in representation-theory research who formulate for the machine the process of problem solving; related to this is heuristic (trial-and-error) programming in which the machine system is designed to respond to stochastic (random) variables; robotics goes into what its name suggests—instruments and machines that control themselves and their processes in complex environments.

As far out as any of this research are the efforts to communicate directly with the machine in natural human language. The language natural to machines—the only language they can be said to know—is binary logic or arithmetic. Instructions and executions work on the simple on-or-off, digital, mode of the computer's circuits and switches. This is machine language. There are no words as words or numbers as numbers as we know them in machine language, only the combinations of 0s and 1s (zeros and ones in binary). To make the machine "understand," to instruct it and have it execute the program, arithmetic and human language have to be encoded into binary, and usually this is accomplished by first turning human instructions into higher-level languages like Fortran, Cobol or PL/1. The machine itself then matches these codes to machine language and proceeds to instruct itself, execute, and communicate or record the results. As long as we work with *digital* computers, and speed and flexibility seem to secure them in the job for the foreseeable future, this translation into machine language will be a must.

Language, then, direct from the user to the machine or abstracted several times from the source or input, is fundamental to electronic cognition. Perhaps the most important research into language and the computer has been done at Massachusetts Institute of Technology (MIT), where linguists such as Noam Chomsky have been working since the 1950s on a machine-oriented approach to grammar. The intention has been to have the computer generate sentences in English that are both grammatical and acceptable—two qualities that purists may be distressed to learn are not identical in the domain of the new grammar. For all Chomsky's effect on linguistics, and it has been revolutionary, no one has succeeded in getting his theories to work on machines. The work goes on, and others at MIT, among them Terrence Winograd, have reported that the computer there has performed some functions equivalent to a human's understanding of language.

In Chomsky's work and elsewhere (W. V. Quine, for instance) there are references to a theory of machines and computability which had been formulated by Alan M. Turing and others in the 1930s. This has to do with the fitting of strings of logical statements into patterns that can produce valid deductions in machines. Chomsky's effort has been to observe and deduce the rules for what takes place when a man transforms what underlies the expression into what is said, and to state these rules in computable form.

How logical is man even at his most brilliant? How logical therefore can be his machines? Turing had suggested that a machine could be said to think when what it says cannot be distinguished from what a human speaker can be expected to say in a similar conversation.

Shortfalls in artificial-intelligence experiments might prove nothing more than the imperfectibility of logic and language. The rules have always been changing. Perhaps machines will be more truly said to think the more closely they approach the inefficient and imperfect efforts of man's brain. Man's use of sounds and the connections between them, and of ideas and their connections, is marvelous *and* correctible. Who's to say that machines can't work with the uncertain as well as man can? Let's say "their guess is as good as yours" so long as the uncertainty is retained as a weighted part of any offered "decision."

The work of Bell Labs is to the point. The auditory-research department there, under the direction of James L. Flanagan, can be said to have taught a computer to convert English text—the North Wind story and other snatches of prose—into synthetic speech. They combined a computer model of the human speech apparatus—lips, teeth, soft palate, tongue, vocal cords, nasal cavity—with a stored dictionary that contained words in a digital code based on the speech sounds and pauses that form them. When they "fed" printed sentences to the machine, it "read" the words and produced by electronic conversion the appropriate sounds with inflections that closely resembled actual speech.

Sampled-data theory is at work here. According to Flanagan, writing in *Scientific American* (February 1972), sampled-data theory "tells one how to represent the behavior of continuous physical systems . . . in terms of discrete numerical operations." The electronic model of the mouth and of the physical events that produce speech represent something not easy to explain. And with Votrax, as used in the General Electric Information Service and in aircraft as spoken warnings ("Pull up! Pull up!"), we come to a real-world simulation of intelligence—the computer able to form words and speak them. There's a sense here of dealing with an x-factor in intelligence, an unknown happening in the mind when knowing takes place. All these systems—the Bell Lab synthesizer, Votrax, and man—make the connection between discrete changes in utterance on the one side and meaning on the other. A combination of the sounds (phonemes) that form the word *wind,* for instance, means "wind." The stored dictionary so informs the system, making the connection between the printed word and the sounds and meaning they signify.

There's a program at MIT utilizing a computer as a psychiatrist. The computer, named Eliza, from Shaw's *Pygmalion* and Lerner and Loewe's *My Fair Lady,* is programmed:

PLEASE TELL ME YOUR PROBLEM
I'm feeling depressed
HOW LONG HAVE YOU BEEN FEELING DEPRESSED?
Ever since my mother left
TELL ME MORE ABOUT YOUR FAMILY
My father is very strict
PLEASE GO ON
Last night I dreamed he spanked me
WHAT WOULD IT MEAN TO YOU IF HE SPANKED YOU?
Didn't you ever get spanked?
WE WERE DISCUSSING YOU, NOT ME
You're just a dumb machine anyway
DO COMPUTERS FRIGHTEN YOU?

If one is satisfied to deal with a psychiatrist by way of a keyboard I/O terminal, this seems at first glance to satisfy

Turing's test requirements. It might well be a discussion with a real psychiatrist. The computer seems to understand what the patient has said, and even seems to apply a certain amount of psychiatric interview technique. Actually, the program uses a very simple system of patterns containing key words. Whenever it receives a statement in the form "I am . . . ," it responds, "How long have you been . . . ?" and fills in the end of its answer from the end of the patient's original statement. When the program receives the word *mother,* it says, "Tell me more about your family." The patterns are set up to reflect a certain amount of psychiatric knowledge. For example, one response to "I dreamed that . . ." is "Do you often wish that . . . ?"—operating on Freud's principle that dreams are wish-fulfillment. When the program receives the word *everyone,* it asks, "Who in particular can you think of?" This tends to elicit a description of a situation that the person at first was reluctant to detail. With a large store of such patterns, the program can carry on an extended dialogue without repeating.

The program's knowledge is in scattered fragments, though, and it has no real understanding of what the patient says. If the patient happens to type, "Thinking about what I am doing always upsets me," Eliza blindly applies the patter for "I am . . ." and comes up with "How long have you been doing always upsets you?" If "she" fails to find one of the key words, the program launches into endless loops of "Please go on," "Tell me more," and so on. And, most important, the program doesn't build up a picture of what the patient is saying. It merely reacts to each sentence according to the particular words that appear in it. Joseph Weizenbaum, who created Eliza, sought to demonstrate that very little understanding is necessary for a machine to appear competent. The program's flaws are due not to its size or to the patterns in its storage, but to its inability to attempt true comprehension. A real psychiatrist needs a huge storehouse of knowledge about people, and especially about his patients, their pasts, thoughts and activities. He also needs a highly developed reasoning power in order to combine this knowledge in a comprehensible manner. We are only beginning to explore the means to represent such a knowledge in a computer; we have only the most rudimentary way of having the machine use it.

Some theorists, taking a leaf, or frame, from the film *2001: A Space Odyssey*, seem determined to build feelings into the machines that exhibit artificial intelligence. No matter; thinking goes on in man without feeling, sometimes to his benefit, sometimes not, and so it will in computers. Regardless too of how rudimentary, thinking is thinking. If the computers aren't thinkers, they nonetheless, even the micros with an array of a thousand-plus binary digits, do the jobs that thinkers do. They are memories; they store and associate the ideas, the data, they contain.

Several prototype systems under study at MIT on grants from the U.S. Navy are robots that can survey their environment and move about, not only seeing by means of TV and hearing but also responding to touch. These automatons demonstrate the possibility that, remotely controlled by computer, they may be able to supplement men, or even in some cases to replace them, in repetitive tasks in hostile, dangerous or stressful surroundings.

Maybe some of the difficulty in understanding the true "mental" characteristics of the computer is that neurological science, the study of the brain and the nervous system, has still a long way to go and many paths to explore. The brain is not fully understood, so comparisons of machine systems with it can hardly be satisfactory. Where intelligence begins, possibly even in the nervous system, is not easy to determine. Take the following about Pavlov's research in *Explorers of the Brain* by Leonard A. Stevens:

Regardless of what was dropped into a dog's mouth, the secretory glands were capable of assessing the material and providing the right juices. Pavlov pointed out that quartz pebbles placed in a dog's mouth prompted no salivation while the animal moved them around and then spat them out. But the same pebbles ground into sand and placed into the dog's mouth caused a liberal flow of watery saliva to help the animal eject the fine particles and clean his mouth. The system was so remarkably purposeful that it seemed "to imply intelligence" in the involved glands, said Pavlov.

No need to accept the implication, except figuratively. Still, salivation, as a servoprocess, comes close to satisfying the requirements of the definition of thinking. ". . . Intellectual exercise leaves residual changes in the brain," Stevens summarizes elsewhere, and these residual changes, one might assume, in the sensory system of the dog, as in the highest centers of the human brain, are the vectors of response—in the one of instinctive reflex and in the other of instructive memory.

According to some, any organization—social, industrial or biological—is an information network. The task is to understand the flow of information in whatever we deem worthy of study and control. Whether such a network must contain a brain, it is certain that thinking and knowing must take place if the information is to be of any consequence. Computers operate beyond the speed and capacity of human brains, and they do the jobs of thinkers, whatever names we give them, or whatever human attributes.

It is not belittling to recognize that the inner workings of a computer are more orderly than the biological brain. How often do you "block" (have a name on the tip of your tongue, or lose the thread of a story)? The computer, receiving instructions and executing a number of programs at the same time, "looks" for a new job just as it "looks" for a new instruction within a single program. The computer can reallocate its own resources to meet the changing demands of each job.

One of the interesting side-effects of computer work is

the discipline it imposes on its users. Discipline is not necessarily conditioning, or punishment, or tyranny. To make this sure, the overriding aim of those in and out of computer technology will have to be to fully value the quantities that refuse to be numbered willy-nilly in the loop of information-processing systems. Good order and discipline imply a recognition of limits by all concerned.

chapter 00010

To Help or Not to Help—
For Better or Worse

The computer as brain, near-brain, extension of brain—whatever—is an intelligent instrument of reason. But, it's no mechanophobic delusion to see it also being turned to unreasonable ends. It's natural that many people, faced with the onslaught of computerization, seek protection from its abuses. With experts and professionals themselves finding it difficult to keep up with new developments, it's not paranoia or unreason which stimulates our anxiety, but real evidence of computer-encroachment into every aspect of our lives. Central to our rising feelings of distrust and dismay is an examination of the role computers play in the crucial areas of privacy and individual rights.

Online and uptight

Orwell's Big Brother was not absent from Senator Sam J. Ervin's committee hearings on the Privacy Bill of 1974. The bill and the hearings focused on the computer and the technological paraphernalia of espionage—the bug, the tap, the automatic-surveillance camera. A 1973 report of the committee cited former Attorney General John Mitchell as having fostered invasions of privacy by increasing the government's use of wire-tapping and by pressing for practices like preventive detention and "no-knock" police entries. Mitchell, the report said, "greatly expanded federal surveillances of citizens thought to be threats to internal security, justifying his action on the theory that the executive has inherent and discretionary power to protect itself." The committee report continued:

> Computerization has made . . . excesses particularly tempting. The collection and computerizing of information by government must be tempered with an appreciation of the basic rights of the individual, of his right to privacy, to express himself freely and associate with whom he chooses. . . . After all, the loss of anonymity, occasioned by having an opinion or an association recorded, creates a climate of subtle coercion.

In Oceania in *1984* Big Brother's face was everywhere, always that bigger-than-life presence, the heavy black mustache, the ruggedly handsome features, and "eyes that follow you about when you move." In today's Superindustrial Society, as Toffler calls it, Big Brother puts on many faces or he is faceless. The credit bureaus and insurance investigation services look, to many, suspiciously like him, or suggest his presence. Some of these operations, especially the credit files, are highly computerized; detailed reports on applicants for insurance (the gumshoe side of the business) are processed and stored manually. The Fair Credit Reporting Act (FCRA) of 1971 regulates dissemination and access to identified files, computer or not, but individual access is still circumscribed and not fully guaranteed by the legislation. The potentialities for abuse are not negligible. Files can be out of date, misleading; they can get into the wrong hands. With all the good will in the world, companies in this field, like the leader, Equifax, Inc. (the name was changed from Retail Credit Co. in 1975), recognize their vulnerability. They are beset with litigation, live under its cloud. The 1974 Annual Report of Retail Credit proudly announced a new policy of openness, going beyond the letter of the Act in allowing access. Interestingly, though, for all the protective measures in the FCRA, the consumer who wants to challenge his record in a credit file is not entitled to know the source of the supposedly wrong information.

The social security number (SSN) has become in the United States the nearest thing to a universal identifier. It simplifies filing and processing for any institution, agency or firm that must maintain files of individually identified information. However, it vastly simplifies also the interchange of data between files and clearly can interfere with an individual's right to protect information about himself and to handle his own money and other affairs with the least interference. The U.S. Privacy Act of 1974 was passed without an amendment covering a person's right to refuse to give his SSN to a government bureau, but future legislation is possible. From an administrative point of view, eliminating or lessening the use of the SSN, license numbers and other such identifiers would raise serious problems. For universities alone, which use the SSN in their computers, to convert their records in order to file under a different, less maneuverable system, say alphabetical, the costs would be impossible to estimate. Meanwhile, the individual grasps whatever straws may blow his way. Incomputability may become a fourth unalienable right.

All the legislation so far—the Family Educational Rights and Privacy Act of 1974, the Privacy Act, the FCRA, and others—as well as what's bound still to come in Washington and in the states—points to the complexity of the issues, to the widespread concern and to the variety of interests looking for remedies or for things to remain as they are. It's interesting that Sweden was able to tie it all together in one piece of legislation—the Data Act of 1973. But Sweden's a small country. With almost twenty-five times her population, the United States, were it to enact twenty-five times the legislation, would doubtless still leave its citizenry unsure of its footing in matters of privacy and access to information.

The jealous love of privacy and fear of an overweening bureaucracy run smack into efforts at control which many consider essential. Typical is the opposition to PSRO ("professional standards review organizations," or peer review), a system whereby state and local medical authorities can review and evaluate the level of health care in their communities. Such conflicts only point up the tension between personal and social interests, a tension that is sharpened by the immediacy and multiplication of information sources. Computers naturally play a large role in PSROs and in related programs like Medicare, Medicaid and any of the proposals for a national health insurance plan. To opponents of PSRO the process can be sinister. Hospital authorities fill out questionnaires on each patient. The questionnaires identify patients, doctors, diagnosis, treatment, and length of stay, and the resulting information is fed to the computer. Any extraordinary things about the case are "kicked out" in an exception report—changes in the accepted routines, longer-than-usual confinement to bed, that sort of thing. The local peer review groups can then go over the exceptions with staff members involved, accept the deviations, or take steps to correct faults and abuses. No manual filing procedure could approach the computer's success in handling such masses of detail. Statistics relate to costs, kinds of drugs, medical and surgical procedures, and types of patients by age, income, and insurance coverage; interrelating these data allows the group and the government to oversee health care in ways never before possible. To some the computer's a policeman; to others it's a reasonable, sensitive set of alarms.

The number of interlocking computer networks is stunning. More astonishing are those that could be interlocked were it not for congressional and public resistance. The FBI has fingerprints on 86 million people; a program for putting these on computer is under way. The bureau's National Crime Information Center (NCIC) receives arrest data from police agencies throughout the country and transmits information on demand to the thousands of terminals that are hooked up to its central processing units. The Selective Service system has a magnetic-tape file containing information on all persons subject to the draft. The federal income tax files, the census, social security, Medicare and Medicaid, all the state welfare agencies, tax and real estate commissions, mental health, motor vehicle, birth, marriage and death records exist in autonomous computer storage. There are obvious cost-effective reasons for these to be combined in one massive network hooked into a national data bank (like FEDNET, a serious proposal shot down in large part by the disclosures of the Ervin committee), or in lesser federations of networks. However, love of privacy is no pipe dream. When straightforward congressional investigation (like that under Robert Kastenmeier, chairman of the House Civil Liberties Subcommittee) comes up with 10,000 instances of mail surveillance in the 1973–74 period, any revival of schemes like FEDNET would be in for heavy going. Surveillance of the "surveillers" seems difficult enough when they have to confine their work to traceable "mail covers" and court-ordered "openings." What might it become were not only law enforcement and intelligence, but also the Postal Service, the departments of Agriculture and Labor, the Fish and Wildlife Service, and the myriad state agencies, who were cited in the hearings for the alleged abuses of mail, able to ply their trade in the security of an interagency sharing of computer files?

Sinking the float

Rising computerization on a more personal scale reveals that as simple a procedure as handling a bank account suddenly promises to slip from our hands. The Social Security system began in 1971–72 to experiment with transferring payments to beneficiaries' accounts in Florida and Georgia. No monthly payment check was needed, conjuring prospects of untold administrative savings. The system calls upon the beneficiary to open a bank account or to have the deposits forwarded to the account he already has. This was an early incursion of EFTS (electronic funds transfer system), which was to spread considerably by 1975. Through computers and communications hookups, EFTS transfers money from an account at one point to an account at another—between two or more banks, between a store and a bank or between an individual and a bank. In the spring of 1975, within a span of several months, fourteen commercial banks in nine states and a hundred-odd savings-and-loan associations in seventeen states had installed EFTS or notified banking authorities that they intended to do so. In a typical instance, you might appear at a supermarket checkout with your groceries and tell the clerk you wanted to withdraw money from your savings bank in order to pay your bill. The clerk would enter the withdrawal authorization on a keyboard which is part of a minicomputer, a small specialized processing and sending unit no bigger, as they say in "Twenty Questions," than a bread box. This unit, by direct electronic connection, queries the bank's file on your account and, when all is in order, authorizes the market to collect what's coming to it and give you the change, if any. In the process your account would be debited, and the market's account, or its bank, if it's different from yours, would be credited. The whole transaction would take little more time than simply your handing the clerk the cash, certainly less time than writing a check and having the check approved.

On the face of it, EFTS is a boon to the consumer. Apart from disemploying bank tellers, retail clerks and any number of others, the system stands to do to the check what the check did to currency—take over the job of paying bills. However, people will be deprived of the "float"—checks in the process of clearing for collection. An "insufficient funds" notice will be zapped to the vendor instantaneously, without the payer having his usual chance, as is sometimes welcome and part of the game plan, to run to the bank to cover the float.

EFTS admittedly shatters no worlds; one can retain his routines if he chooses, and continue to pay by check, floating to his heart's content, or with cash. Still, it's another ramifying force at work thanks to "smart" electronics. Canada, for instance, is enough concerned with electronic funds transfer systems and payments by credit and "money" cards to see the need for protective laws. The country's Law Reform Commission released a paper in early 1975 proposing that the public be allowed to take part in setting up new payment systems. Innovation, it's saying, can't be permitted without a vote, or some form of input, from those most affected.

To expect new legislation to be the answer to the problem is rather like the rational gambler who works up a strategy to take to Las Vegas. He knows it's a house game, the only one in town. The best he can do is lose slowly. Likewise, when the individual, with the computer, comes to think he's in "the only game in town," the gradual erosion of personal freedom should come as no surprise. He, we, might be willing to bet that that information has to be on our side, were it not for the instances where it's plainly with "them."

Trust in electronic information, the only game in town, then, becomes a trust in machines. The computer offers itself as an instrument of reason, *if* the men who work it, we ourselves, can be controlled and trusted. *If* . . . suspicions of abuse, fraud, surveillance, and hands-off no-fault management of one's own, and one's employer's, affairs take on a villainous look with the machine running a good part of the program. Present laws, Donn B. Parker points out in his *Computer Abuse*, might require replacement with new kinds of laws to reflect the new concepts,

> . . . a change that must be accomplished in the face of impending disaster in business relationships. Computer abuse could go out of control if it were to pass some critical stage. The consequences could lead to social chaos, since there is no turning back to manual systems once the economy and society are geared to advanced levels of automation.

Parker has made a profession of computer security—the study of systems to make them resistant to failure and tampering. He turned from a career in systems analysis to this pioneer specialty out of a concern, he has said, for the ethics of his fellow professionals. Asked what ethics they had, he answered, "None."

Measurable public feeling shows a pretty mixed bag of attitudes—little direct acquaintance, some hope, some suspicion. In one survey, the Canadian Social Survey Research Centre found, among other things, that 12.6 percent of respondents had direct contact with computers and 53.9 percent expect that individuals will eventually have terminals to computers in their homes. Almost half (45 percent) consider the computer accurate; 16 percent think it an intelligent machine. Of this segment, half (8 percent of the total sample) think the computer smarter than the average person; about one in five respondents look upon the computer as just another appliance; 73 percent agreed with the statement, "Computers will give us more leisure time," while only 47 percent felt that this would be accompanied by a higher standard of living. More than half (52 percent) associate computers with violations of confidentiality, and seven of ten felt that serious errors in judgment could result from computers if human factors were not taken into consideration.

IBM, which is estimated to control anywhere from 50 to 70 percent of the world's computer business, emphasizes the instrumental role; data processing systems are meant:

> . . . to *assist* in running enterprises, administering institutions, directing research, and planning future activities. . . . Regardless of the product, or problem, the nature of the enterprise or institution, wherever there is need for information upon which human judgments can be based, there *may* also exist a need for a data processing system. (Italics inserted)

This last is from its *Student Text*, fourth edition, published in 1970. In 1975, in a *New Yorker* advertisement, "IBM Reports: The computer and research," the company sustains the modest tone (italics inserted): "The computer *serves* society . . . *helping* us make better use of our resources. It is a management *tool,* providing [now a little boldly] perspective on complex decisions." We then see the computer, though still instrumental, "re-creating and analyzing interactions that could not otherwise be observed or understood." The ad makes no grand claims about electronic marvels, but weights the division of intellectual labor on the side of the machine! The machine is "performing calculations that were often impractical, or even impossible, only a few short years ago." The message, in the light of besetting antitrust litigation and the hunger of competitors and professionals for the giant's dismemberment, is finally that the company makes "critical contributions" to advances in computer technology—a blessing that all, society and the competition, can benefit from.

Student introductions and mass-media advertisements are unlikely places for warnings about computer abuse, or for pointing up hazards to the social well-being. Gaps of this sort, however, do not indicate that IBM and the industry are insensitive to any general unease or to informed fault-finding like Donn Parker's. IBM's six-volume *Data Security and Data Processing* (1974), for instance, is a good example of their concern with computer abuse. Though divine inspiration is not evident in the language, it has to constitute some sort of bible on the subject. It resulted from two years of work with data processing people in a state government (Illinois), a major university (MIT), a major computer-service organization (TRW Systems), and a federal systems center (the IBM installation in Gaithersburg, Maryland), and it is by no means a whitewash or Pollyanna gloss. From a quick run through it, two things are obvious: (1) there is no foolproof technique or device that will make any computer totally immune from failure and tampering; (2) the reasons this is so are not obvious.

EDP at work

In order to understand these two statements we must first know exactly what a computer does and the uses it's put to. Two good textbooks on the subject are IBM's *Student Text* quoted above, and Gordon B. Davis's *Introduction to Electronic Computers.* Here goes a summary of this material:

The computer holds a program of instructions; it reads data in machine-readable form; it computes some of the data—arithmetic; it manipulates data as symbols and makes comparisons—logic; it retrieves data from its own or peripheral storage—memory—and it outputs (transmits) the new data which its operations have produced. Current large, general-application computers are capable of performing from 10- to 100-million instructions per second (MIPS). There are other measures of computer speed, distinct execution cycles that can occur in nanoseconds, for instance, but MIPS seems the truest and most useful. The machine can be said to operate only as fast as its instruction stream. Succinctly, according to the IBM text:

> Instructions usually consist of at least two parts, an operation and an operand. The operation tells the machine which function to perform: read, write, add, subtract, and so on. The operand can be the address of data or an instruction in main storage, the address of data or programs in secondary storage, or the address of an input/output unit. It can also specify a control function, such as shifting a quantity in a register, or backspacing and rewinding a reel of tape.

It's said that a computer can perform in two minutes what it would take fifty years for a human to do by hand. But such comparisons are meaningless. For one thing, how many additions can a bright schoolboy do in a minute? what kind of addition? in his head or on paper? After twenty minutes of steady going he probably couldn't do any for a while. For another thing, which can't be repeated too often, the enormous speeds of computers create a new mathematics and invite the lengthy, involved analyses that man on his own would never conceive of.

Recordkeeping, the primary and best known job of a computer, may be done in either of two ways. In the first, batch processing, the records and accounts (for payroll, billing, payments, inventory and so forth) are accumulated and done in sequence at the end of a workday, or weekly or monthly, whenever a supply of related information builds up and must be entered into the records and the updated results printed out. The other means of recordkeeping, online realtime (OLRT) processing, allows documents and transactions to be entered as they appear, singly, without having to wait for more of the same. A number of sources, therefore, can feed information from terminals in separate departments and branches and the offices of subscribers, customers or suppliers without the users interfering one with the other. Each input changes the total of information in each user's file, and each file is thereby kept continuously up to date. You operate in realtime when you can be said to get back information in time to act on it. And you are online when all the storage, files and terminals are connected to the central processing unit (CPU) and capable of responding to any proper command at any time. Typical of OLRT installations are airline reservations systems and the depositors' records in a savings bank.

Recordkeeping in both batch and online modes is a straightforward office function, but with the possibilities that computers offer for interrelating data—payroll or inventory, for instance, as functions of cost and scheduling—recordkeeping takes on an immediately global character within an organization. And with OLRT not only clerks and managers, but also terminals that may be part of metering instruments in factories, laboratories or hospitals, can input information. Either way or both, such complex recordkeeping provides the means for the CPU and managers to gain instant and periodic profiles on what the system is up to.

Beyond these "primitive" uses are higher levels of performance. One example is simulation (pages 22–24). Another is linear programming (LP). Indeed, for all its complexity, LP is one of the first uses computers were put to. The Air Force's Project SCOOP (Scientific Computations of Optimum Programs), for instance, arose from the impulse after World War II to study the most efficient means of allocating the material and human resources of the country in the event of total war. The concurrent development of the computer offered a way to store and manipulate the vast arrays of information and formulas involved. Economist Wassily Leontieff had constructed an input-output model that charts the interrelationship of all the industry sectors of the United States—the dollar volume of sales to and purchases from each. What quantity of chemicals the paper industry buys and how much paper it sells to printers and publishers would be specifics derivable from the chart, and either figure would allow us to determine how much of either commodity—chemicals or paper—is available to the remaining sectors. If, in this example, total paper production is fixed, or changing at a fixed rate, any appreciable change in supply to one sector will produce a proportional inverse change in what remains for the others. Likewise, any increase in total capacity will yield proportionately more paper to each of the sectors. These are linear relationships. An early and still typical use of linear programming in industry is in the management of oil refinery production. Here, the technique derives by formula the best combination of products—from asphalt to medicinal spirits—to be got from the best combination of crude-oil input and refinery settings. Factors such as market prices, fractionating heats and pressures are matched to produce the optimum schedule. As with Leontieff's first model in linear programming, the mathematical expressions take advantage of the unique more-than, less-than routing of magnetic changes through a computer.

PERT (program evaluation and review technique) and CPM (critical path method) are related or combined techniques for determining schedules. Designing the elevator system for the World Trade Center in New York was virtually a start-from-scratch affair. Data from other skyscrapers had little real bearing on the elevators for anything as large as the two 110-story towers. Simulation by computer allowed Otis (the supplier of the equipment) to match the speed and capacity of cars and escalators with space limitations and expected flows of passenger traffic under all predictable conditions. The result: 254 elevators and 68 escalators in the two towers to carry 50,000 workers and

80,000 daily visitors. Try that on your slide rule and wall charts. Critical path method then generated the optimum schedule for the manufacture and delivery of the materials in order to match the timing of the rest of the construction: not to have deliveries waiting overlong to be unloaded on busy downtown streets, not to be late and delay other work, not to have delivered equipment sitting around before shaftways were ready.

PERT and CPM combine in a program all the steps that have to be taken (events that have to take place) for a job or project to reach completion. A network is formed to include all the steps and to display the best sequence relating one step to the others. PERT not only serves to set up a schedule but also may serve to monitor and change the continuing operation.

Other higher-level computer functions are information retrieval, as in a system like the *New York Times* Information Bank, which makes extracts of articles from the *Times* and fifty-odd magazines available by means of typed requests at a terminal keyboard, a search of data storage by the computer, and the projection of the ordered extracts on the terminal CRT; computer-assisted programmed learning, in which the student uses a terminal to interact with a text on any number of subjects; decision simulation, in which a computer "scores," tests or tries out decisions that participants in strategy or management games make in solving problems.

Management information system (MIS) is an elaborate application of both basic and advanced computer techniques. Fundamentally, MIS applies the sum of an organization's computer information to the making of decisions of the highest order. There is a data base that is online realtime; it records all transactions as they occur and are entered by all the functions in the system; it contains all history or backup and the rules for decisions. There is a monitoring system to mark events and trends that have to be bucked on to the person or function responsible; a system of priorities and routings for reports and displays, as well as a system that authorizes requests for special reports. Finally, there's decision simulation for the testing of possible outcomes. MIS is a far-ranging effort to integrate men and machines and to interrelate functions. It has proved difficult to implement, yet it continues as a goal or ideal for the complex organization.

In medicine, the uses of computers become ever more involved and involving. Many hospitals have automated the business side of their recordkeeping—billing, purchasing and payroll—but they are also scheduling staff, facilities, and outpatient visits, and they are beginning to computerize case histories, as well as to centralize by computer the monitoring and control of intensive-care systems and units. There are experimental programs for assisting in diagnosis. The doctor may input the symptoms and indications of a case and receive back from the data storage of the computer extracts on all the illnesses associated with the set of circumstances he's presently concerned with. A physician's memory and experience are not replaced but supplemented by the infinitely greater store of associations in the computer's storage. It's not farfetched to speculate on the utility of simulation models as tests of a set of alternatives in treatment.

Whatever dangers the expansion of computer technology may hold for us, we can be sure of one thing: change. Constant, exciting, spectacular change. The next decades will hurl us into crises as fascinating and dangerous as any generation has faced in the entire span of mankind. It doesn't matter to this coming world whether we believe in it, whether we fear it, whether we welcome it. Inevitably, a computer society will come. Indeed, much of it is already with us. One sensible thing to do is to admit its presence and to figure out ways to live with it. If we've learned anything in our life on earth, from the days we first snatched fire from nature, or used our earliest slingshot to bring down a distant enemy, or tilled the soil with the remotest ancestor of the modern plow—then we'd better put that accumulated wisdom to work in this impending age.

Technical change has already given many of us too much to swallow too fast. The adjustment to the rapidity and the scope of computer-magnified upheavals may be costly and painful. There's an enormous mismatch between the acceleration of technology and social readiness. It's hard not to try to avoid the chaos of the transition: it seems that there must be a way to plan and prepare. Yet there's the relentless expansion in numbers of units installed and the astronomical increase in computing power. Toffler writes:

> Social rationality presupposes individual rationality, and this in turn depends not only on certain biological equipment, but on continuity, order, and regularity in the environment. It is premised on some correlation between the pace and complexity of change and man's decisional capacities. By blindly stepping up the rate of change, the level of novelty, and the extent of choice, we are thoughtlessly tampering with these environmental preconditions of rationality. We are condemning countless millions to future shock.

Without preparation, there will be vacuums aplenty that freebooters from government and commerce may be only too happy to fill. With preparation, government and commerce can be kept responsive to everyone's needs: starting and ending, in the computer age, with the bricks and mortar of knowledge and reason electronically available to all and at the lowest cost in time, fees and energy.

Less than ten years ago, there were some 50,000 computers in use. Only the very largest organizations needed them—banks, universities, government bureaus, big factories—and were using them effectively. Very few others —individuals, smaller enterprises, schools and shops— found computers vital to their livelihood. All this has meanwhile changed. Computers have fallen drastically in price; a dollar's worth of computer time buys up to twenty times more in 1976 than it did ten years ago. (What happened to Grosch's law?) Today practically every business, factory or plant, school, government office, retail store, hospital, hotel, laboratory—you name it—finds some need for a computer in order to keep up or stay competitive. (The corner butcher has two scales; the new one gives out in light-emitting diodes [LEDs] the weight, the price per pound and the total cost. This scale is a smart terminal; its brain is a microcomputer, a semiconductor chip, able to perform the arithmetic in the time it takes the butcher or his wife to add a slice of ham to the pan of the scale.) About 1,700 of the large computers (or mainframes, as they're sometimes called) were shipped monthly to customers by American firms in 1975; more than 4,000 a month of the small machines, the minicomputers (often called minis, and when they start to encroach on the large systems, megaminis); and it's impossible to give a meaningful count of the microprocessing units like that in the butcher's scale. The number of mainframes and minicomputers installed at the start of 1975 was estimated at 266,000.

With all this, what of the workaday measures to establish controls, controls tied in practical ways to the confidence and regularity so acutely felt to be needed? *Data Security and Data Processing,* the IBM study, is properly down to earth, hedging a bit, yet assigning no little share of responsibility to the industry for maximizing control.

> Individuals in advanced industrialized nations today expect, as a matter of course, services that were once far beyond the reach of their forebears. Higher education, social security, workmen's compensation, instant credit, insurance coverage of all kinds—these have become the hallmarks of the humane society. But no organization—public or private—can administer these services unless it continuously collects, updates and verifies information about the people it has been authorized to serve.

Business organizations today must cope with greater volumes of information than ever before. If management is to make sound decisions, it must have accurate and timely information about its operations. To gain access to current data, many firms are implementing management information systems that consolidate large amounts of information in common data bases. The centralized files represent a risk, for these critical business records may either be inadvertently destroyed or fall into the wrong hands.

Practical security for a device of management: "What's good for General Motors [read IBM, TRW, HEW, whichever you like of the other 476,305 two-, three-, and four-letter acronyms] is good for . . . ," etc. The peril afflicts the served and the serving. So far so good with regard to privacy and whatever other fears the bogey of consumerism can raise in the minds of the establishment. If we don't clean up ourselves, seems the message, there might be no single Ralph Nader or one troop of "raiders," but legions of them, and we'll be up to our I/Os in litigation, boycotts, legislation. Invasions of privacy and the attendant abuses—fraud, sabotage, espionage, bureaucratic shoddiness—might not be widely enough recognized as dangers, but at least they often make the network news when they occur. The other danger, disemployment, and its attendant abuse, indifference, is neither obvious nor amenable, as are the others, to ready means of correction. In a time of high unemployment (nearing 10 percent in 1975), who takes the time to pick through the dross to separate the technologically displaced from the generalized victims of global rollbacks? The man or woman out of work because of cost-effective data processing and automation is social pollution of the highest (worst) sort, negative feedback at its most alarming.

Maybe privacy is not the paramount issue. Maybe control is more important—control within the machines, control over the machines and control over the people who run them.

Self-discipline, used car salesmen, other trusted guardians

In early 1971, testifying before the Subcommittee on Constitutional Rights, the then Assistant Attorney General and later Supreme Court Justice William Rehnquist took the position that Congress has no business concerning itself with wire-tapping and computerized records. "I think it quite likely that self-discipline on the part of the Executive branch will provide an answer to virtually all of the legitimate complaints against excesses of information-gathering."

The legitimate complaints Americans have about information-gathering and dissemination have much to do with the lack of self-discipline on the part of many people and institutions. Complaints also stem from the insufficiency of legislation that spells out what rights each of us has with regard to the records kept on us. Government and business, the press and broadcasting, the computer service bureaus, as well as hospitals, universities and the foundations—information brokers all—drone away electronically at the facts and figures, the stuff that the superindustrial "we" is made of. The onetime second to John Mitchell had his lofty assessment of executive self-discipline; reasonable men have theirs.

What this massive processing of persons means is that (1) a record in a computer file is no longer a single entity—it extends and modifies the data it's made a part of; (2) it is itself changed by its vulnerability to change and interaction with data outside its own surroundings; and (3) it subjects the individual it represents to manipulations and modifications which, by his absence, he is not a party to. A computer is not infallible, though it has to be treated as such for its work or results to have any meaning. Yet by their nature, the abbreviations and digital shorthand, the codes of programming, jam people into categories that are imprecise and easy to misuse. Such records may determine one's eligibility for welfare, education, housing, for virtually any public transaction. As cited previously, we are given no notice that our record is in a file, or of what rights we may have to examine the contents.

Few mechanisms exist for an individual to contest the accuracy or relevance of the information about him in public records. There's a double standard. The individual is expected, often sworn, not to lie or misrepresent; there's no formal return of the pledge by the organization he's dealing with. There are few workable or published rules to govern the sharing of information between files and organizations.

Without effective legislation to protect individual rights, and even with it perhaps, it's no wonder the citizen who gives any thought to the matter feels powerless in the face of computerized decision making. He gets no information about such procedures. He has no voice in them. He has precious little appeal against their unwanted consequences. These feelings have led to continued pressures for new and amended legislation. Congressmen Koch of New York and Barry Goldwater, Jr.; senators Buckley, Ribicoff and Proxmire are among the many—not always a majority, alas—who so effectively carry the banner first fashioned by Sam Ervin, who retired in 1974. Yet, all of these official efforts will be fruitless without public attention from all sides and political persuasions. Regulation won't come without the demand for it. Resistance to change on the part of banks, government bureaus, insurance companies, and the credit and investigative services is forceful and self-protective. As so often in noninstitutional causes (like the environmental crusade), reason and the burden of proof seem to have to rest with the petitioner. As Jerry M. Rosenberg puts it, furthermore, in *The Death of Privacy* (1969):

No attempt shall be made to deny the value of data collection or deny the worth of computerization. The point of concern is that without sufficient effort to inject adequate safeguards, we may some day stop asking whether our privacy is being invaded—when that time arrives we will find that we have no privacy left to invade.

Beyond the threats to privacy, we see the integrity of our institutions and a person's conception of self disappearing. In the face of organizations and machine systems that are not being controlled in the widest interest, what is the individual to do? The forces are pervasive and fugitive.

The Court of Appeals for the District of Columbia, on April 23, 1974, ordered the FBI to expunge a person's arrest record from its NCIC (National Crime Information Center) files if the arrested person was exonerated and released without charges. The FBI had contended that it was merely the depository of criminal records and that the states feeding the files had the obligation for accuracy and updating, never mind the uses they were being put to.

As Thomas Whiteside points out in his quietly devastating "A Reporter at Large: Anything Adverse" in *The New Yorker* (April 21, 1975), insurance companies pass the buck for accuracy on to the independent investigating agencies that check on the insurability of applicants for coverage. What the whole seamy system amounts to is that the underwriters don't want bad witnesses in court cases. All the "moral" determinants of declinability relate only to the applicant as a potential defendant in a liability action. Will he or she look "right" to a jury? Clergymen are too forgiving, they're too ready to share blame; unmarried women are vulnerable to slander; blacks and people with accents are stereotyped as bad risks. So the insurance companies foster a system that thrives on, grinds out quotas of adverse reports. Equifax, Inc., mentioned previously, and hundreds of others exist to give their clients, the insurance companies, what they are after. The companies, Whiteside makes clear, thereby insulate themselves against charges of violating the Fair Credit Reporting Act or of trading in hearsay. Incidentally, a "catch 22" in the process is that the act of exercising one's rights under the FCRA to correct credit or investigative files may be enough to reclassify a person as declinable. The insurance company's interest is to keep down payments to settle suits against the people they cover; they want no oddballs in the courtroom. Actuarially, this may be sound. (It's not, contends Whiteside.) Where it leaves the citizen, he states, is with

> . . . no Constitutional rights worth mentioning . . . ; for the most part, such rights tend to be mere impediments, to be avoided by the application of systems of "protective" and "declinable" information quotas. The citizen unfortunate enough to belong to a disfavored class or category has been tried, judged, and penalized far in advance of any justice that might be obtainable in court.

It is interesting to note that this process of checking into the "morals" of applicants for insurance is not yet computerized. It's a debasing donkey-work system that sends over 5,000 Equifax people a day into the field to collect 150,000 reports on individuals—that's thirty reports a day. (Whiteside puts the usual quota at closer to twenty.) Twenty or thirty, the "field" work would have to be largely by phone, some on-site interviews with neighbors and applicants, references to old reports and, in the case of Equifax, to their computerized bank of credit data.

With all good intentions, computer professionals cannot correct these inequities by applying tight security of access to their computer systems, even were they handling, as they're not, all the backup information. Plainly, the problem with credit rating and insurance investigating, as with so much other information brokering, is the insularity of the users; their blindness to the risks; their sense of being legally sheltered from responsibility for the accuracy of the data they process, by machine or not.

Yet the computer takes the brunt of the outrage and suspicion. Whiteside quotes W. Lee Burge, president of Equifax:

So this investigative process is really one that allows business to broaden its scope, from a marketing standpoint. The whole purpose . . . is to do business according to a fair and equitable arrangement. The reason we've come under criticism is really a lack of public understanding. Many people fear what we do largely because of technological advances—the use of computerized information, and so on. This computer fear is almost a psychosis. American civilization, our total society, is based on a premise of knowledge and freedom of information—the right to know. What's involved in our business is the question of striking the proper balance between the right to know and the right to privacy. We feel that the businessman has a right to know whatever factors may be pertinent to the transactions he is considering. These are the rules of the road that we in this company have followed for the seventy-five years of our existence, and now some of the rules are under question.

Because of the computer? Because of the instantaneousness of information that has accompanied the miniaturization of the electronic circuit in both communications and computer technology? Perhaps. Because it is so pervasive and cheap, information is the first and only commodity of business enterprise that is its own critic. Consumerism rides on information, on the right to know, every bit as much as do Mr. Burge and his customers in the insurance business. It's no surprise that "rules are under question." With all the difficulties before us, though, in exercising the right to know, we may just give up and become mithridatized: made, like the Pontian king Mithridates, slowly immune to poison through a slow diet of the killing potion.

The containment of threats

Privacy and human dignity are the concerns of the individual and of society, and the equitable, secure use of information should be the concern of the organizations that take or earn the right to use it. On the working level, the basic threats to information within computer systems are (1) generalized equipment failure, (2) fire, (3) water damage, (4) errors and omissions, (5) dishonesty, (6) mischief and sabotage, and (7) infiltration. The last three, and especially the last, are perhaps the most intriguing on a suspense-story level. "But," according to *Data Security*, "information can usually be obtained in much less complicated ways. For that reason, protection against elegant methods of intrusion does not constitute a first line of defense."

What are the security measures taken in the industry to insure against these threats to information-gathering? In general, an operating system (still tracking *Data Security*) must isolate its various users from one another. The parts of a system are kept separate and made not to communicate with other parts except as agreed among the users. *Isolation* calls for the setting up of program barriers, between users, and between individual users and any specialized routines in the operating system. With the progress that has been made in multiprocessing—the coordination of two or more systems—and in the use of multiplex channels, keeping users separate is difficult but essential. "Every path to resources is a potential path for accidental or malicious compromise. . . . Normally . . . barriers will be redundant, but when accidents or malicious penetration attempts occur, the barriers will act as firewalls and will either prevent or contain the resulting damage." (F. M. Stepczyck in Volume 4.) Redundancy is a widely used term of the art. In general it refers to a control (as in this quotation) or a check procedure whose absence would not affect the results or shut down a process, but also whose presence makes sure that functions are in order and stay working in the case of failure.

Controlled access, we find, is the technique for policing the cooperation among users in shared systems. It establishes paths through the program barriers on an agreed, selective basis so that common resources remain available as called for. Controlled access balances authorizations with restrictions on those making entries.

Effectiveness of isolation and controlled access depends, not surprisingly, on *identification* and *surveillance.* Identification sets up machine-language names for users, discrete and shared programs, and the common resources. The established codes are made so that they can't be forged. Surveillance detects and reports all breaches of the security barriers. It monitors the protective mechanisms and so ensures the upkeep of audit trails. Audit trails then permit one to trace violations to the source when they occur. ("Users" in some of the literature are not people or firms but surrogates within the system of the flesh-and-blood users outside. One can conceive of preventive detention as one penalty for the offending bits—shades of Monty Python—in cases of malicious penetration. Redundancy bits might be excised in extreme, recidivist delinquency.)

Fundamental to all security techniques and functions is *integrity.* None of them will work if the operating systems that implement them are unreliable and are not kept in good repair. Security mechanisms must be sufficient to handle correctly all foreseeable situations and to sustain security features during overloads, systems changes, debugging and other interruptions in the general routine.

No security measures are absolute. They can be fail-soft, which maybe is a better, more realistic quality than fail-safe. With this in mind, no one is lulled into an easy trust in chance or in a remote elite. Asked by a TV reporter how buses can be made safety-proof to keep kids who hitch rides on them from falling off and getting hurt, a streetwise Harlem boy said: "Stop makin' 'em."

Electronic politics

While the uses of computers have been generally nonpolitical, at least not directly political, the machines are becoming the economic and political base of superindustrial civilization. The management of recent wars and the creation of powerful electronic weapons and devices demonstrate that computers do serve mightily as primary instruments of social control. Through the automation of surveillance and military force, their potential can seem limitless. They have already come to have immense political and economic power as national and multinational assets. As processors and dispensers of information they can be seen satisfying a malign government's need for conformity and regimentation. It's a vision of the computer as the ultimate weapon. Aside from the obvious utility to tyrants, the function of computers in democracies too can be a source of trouble, even calamity. With computers there can be cold comfort in the interplay of conflicting interests which have dampened all previous fears of dictatorship in countries like the United States. This interplay of interests can become part of a single, controlling program of global import that threatens the very bastions of democracy.

Interests may conflict in such a scenario, but only insofar as the conflict serves the overall purpose. "Controlled" scientists might find it politic not to treat all data alike. Though professing respect for truth and objectivity, scientists can work data into acceptable patterns, either confirming or contradicting them according to plan. They can ignore all other facts as irrelevant; indeed they can't do otherwise if the "adjusted scientific method" is to function. Those co-opted by the global interest will not deal equally or objectively with other hypotheses and fields of inquiry. Only laws, programs and controls pretested by computer, functioning without hitch in this scientific madness and providing results to match predictions, will be permitted. Opposition and contradictions from outside the system stand to be classified inoperative.

Prediction has high utility as a political tool. The increasing power of multiprocessing systems, digesting nationloads of information, can build models of the world. Those with the wherewithal can ride the crest of self-fulfilling prophecies. Life in a computer-controlled technocracy is evolving in complexity to a point beyond the understanding of ordinary mortals. Whence, open invitations to elites, elites that will be the controllers of all input and output, of the mighty processors, and the production machines. It's a madness to be made palatable to you and me by the argument that experts deal only with technical matters that the rest of us don't need to know in detail. This new computable democracy, where the important decisions would be made beyond the reach or scrutiny of the citizen, the facts of life blurred by the "lower-level" language and multiplexing confusions of technology, all takes life in the harmless seed of the computer art. It has become no longer a servant but a powerful force for control. The intended beneficiaries are mystified; they turn off in all ways—off their jobs, off their money, off their environment, off the meager, brave efforts at seeing things as they are—and, ultimately, off the computer in the process.

A favorite myth among PR types in the computer world is about the primitive savage, always at the mercy of an environment (weather, crops, wild animals) that he could neither understand nor control, who was saved by machines and technology. Supposedly the advances of science freed him and us from ignorance and impotence in the face of natural forces. If we stop and think about our situation now, though, we may not be as far along as the so-called savage in this matter of looking after ourselves, of controlling the factors that affect our lives.

Governments govern, and governing has its roots in

steering; steering—manipulating. The best efforts at reform will stink of subjection to someone. The nastiest efforts at subjection can have the sweet smell of reform to others. What distinguishes the two is information. And whether this information is shared or controlled or coerced would seem to determine which, reform or subjection, it will be. Free access to data, under fair guidelines, constitutes a break in information control. No democracy can thrive without it, and no despot can survive with it.

Data become information when they take on meaning for someone and can be subjected to analysis and change. Our ability to make changes in data depends upon their availability to us, whether as individuals we are seeking private knowledge or, through political representatives, seeking an understanding of the forces loose in the world. Control of people is information-based, and information when it's fed in doses fails liberty. Full availability of information provides the spiritual sinews of freedom. Without a wide choice, freedom is a contradiction, literally worthless. That's why efforts to preserve freedom of information can never be allowed to flag.

Computers are the means for simply and speedily automating specificity from out of complexity. Information that counts and is relevant becomes ever more available as microprocessing and "satelliting" of messages progress, inside, outside, between and among computers and users. To what extent will this ore, this enlightening raw material, become a public resource and utility? To what extent will information be kept unblocked to proper inquiry? It would be good to know: secrecy, we continue to have to be taught, is the staple of despots.

On February 19, 1975, several amendments to the Freedom of Information Act of 1966 went into effect. The amendments require the federal government to process requests for information within ten days and to pay court costs if a complainant wins his suit to force disclosure.

Bureaucrats who withhold information against justified claims are subject to penalty, and the courts have the authority to determine whether classifications such as "national security" are justified.

With this lowering of the barriers there was a flood of inquiries to the FBI, the CIA, and the IRS, as well as to the departments of Defense, State and Justice. People were interested in, among many things, tax rulings and investigations, and ratings and reports on products that the government has the authority to regulate. Journalists and other interest groups were, of course, among the petitioners—requesting such information as previously withheld transcripts of press briefings.

The availability of government information made possible through this new legislation gave a great boost to the public's right to know. However, in the area of employment, no such correctives have taken place to ameliorate the new and insidious processes of displacement and disemployment.

The technological deep-freeze

Displacement is the transfer out of a job into another where retraining or dismissal is the choice. Disemployment is termination or firing when a job or function has been taken over by a computer or an automated procedure. We might stop to agree on a definition of automation: it is the making or converting of devices, machines, instruments or processes to perform under specified conditions certain functions without the intervention of a human operator. Decision-making inserters, like those made by Pitney-Bowes, are units that read the code on an invoice and determine what charge slips and advertising flyers are to be put into an envelope; they stuff the envelope, seal it, and meter it for postage. A person might stand by to see that nothing jams, but hands, eyes and brains have been displaced or disemployed. Automation is related to but not synonymous with cybernetics; that's the study, as we've seen, of control apparatus, or feedback systems, in natural and machine processes.

Displacement and disemployment exact an unmeasured toll. The welcome mat is out in any office for labor- and cost-saving equipment. The relief from humdrum, if not soul-destroying and backbreaking, chores should free office people for more creative work. The reality, however, is that what most people are relieved and freed from are opportunities for advancement and any sense of security. Those nagging, nonhuman reminders of one's replaceability, see how they plug in and plug out.

Whatever the effect of the high cost of computers heretofore in keeping down the spread of automation, the proliferation of the microdevices in 1974–75 overnight wiped out cost as a factor. Numerous computer-related techniques, duplicating and copying machines, electromechanical billing and recordkeeping, halve and quarter the work of secretaries. Even the one- and two-person operation, such as a dentist's office, is able to do without clerical assistance. The assistant there is technically trained and, in the case of the dentist's office, does professional work—cleaning, X-raying—and adds to the productivity of the enterprise. Like the elevator operator, whose ups and downs self-service has solved forever, the office assistant, secretary or clerk will retrain for or assume executive functions or find himself or herself treadmilling it in less genteel surroundings.

An understanding of disemployment is clouded by the business cycle. In a time of prosperity, employment is high, but there is inflation. Companies and government are forced to automate to maintain high productivity. Automation keeps a ceiling on employment. In a time of recession there are layoffs. At first glance this is out-and-out unemployment; there are fewer jobs, fewer things to produce and sell, fewer people needed on all levels save the servicing of unemployment claims. When prosperity returns, there are no jobs, or few, for the unemployed, because automation has disemployed them. Technologically related *dis*employment is buried in the neutral, economically related *un*employment. Machines and machined people provide products and services with the return to normal, and millions are "permanently" out in the cold—people of all vocations, training and skills. The disemployed are the permafrost of the superindustrial Siberia.

John Kenneth Galbraith in *The New Industrial State* (1967) sees the class conflict turning from money as the litmus of social standing to education. As before there have been the rich and the poor, there are now the educated and the not educated. Those who are educated have the capital that keeps the juices flowing in the industrial state—information. But do they? Are the educated the proprietors of this new capital? Some, yes; but the educated per se, no. For education itself often fails on one side or the other. Henry Adams is not the last Harvard graduate to think himself short-changed. Perhaps education has been forced to carry too much of the burden. Perhaps it too is *owned* and therefore not dispensing the information that leads to participation in the control of this new treasury. The facts are that a surplus of labor, especially highly sophisticated labor, can often be combined with a severe shortage. The statistical totals of the unemployed have little meaning in this regard, for the demand for technological ability is a shifting thing—now one expertise is required, now another. The educated can stay employed, busy, but with a tenuous free-lance hold on what part of their armamentarium of skills is most saleable at any given time and place.

Kicking the paycheck habit

It's not easy, they say, to break the paycheck habit—the taxes withheld, the medical insurance, the expense account. It's not a womb, but it is protective, that corporate shelter, even for corporation presidents, like the one W. T. Grant fired for poor performance and whom they kept on salary anyway at $100,000 a year. In the usual case, what does the salesman-of-self know that really counts? Many times, only that what he knows is not what has to be known, and that what has to be known is behind barriers he can't penetrate—like the possibility, plausibility, of discrimination against him on the grounds of sex, age, race, the misleading record of past employment, and credit standing. To borrow a phrase, unemployment is much more coercive, and corrosive, than work.

Russell Baker makes some characteristically cogent, not funny this time, observations on unemployment and the work ethic in the *New York Times Magazine* of April 20, 1975. He is prompted by a TV news story of a college student who works as an actress in pornographic films as a way to beat the recession. It seems the success of blue movies has disemployed the uneducated sexual gymnasts. Lines to memorize and concentration—a story line—call for more than venereal prowess in the feature-length product that now packs them in at the skin flicks. This story, together with a poignant piece in the *Times* a few days before by an unemployed family man, recalls to Baker the pieties of Richard Nixon on the work ethic: those on welfare he thought might be better people if they preferred "carrying bedpans to accepting Government money." With the rise in the number of middle-class executives out of work, Baker suggests that the former president's dictum would no longer be so widely applauded.

If the recession [he writes] is forcing us to admit that poverty results from an absence of jobs instead of spiritual deficiency, the country may make a beneficial adaptation to hard times and start asking whether an economic order that requires so many people to choose between bedpans and the dole all their lives is as close to perfection as it is cracked up to be.

The programmed rival

On the job, it's instinctive to look upon a computer as a "work competitor" and as a potential replacement. As a "fellow employee" the computer's speed, reliability, flexibility and dedication to specific tasks make it an irritating, scary rival.

In the broad view, automated plants can't operate below a certain level. Downward trends in demand for the products made have been handled traditionally by downward changes in the number of products turned out and of people employed. With automation, downward adjustments below the efficiency level aren't feasible and plants can't absorb the shocks of lowered output. There's a premium, therefore, on being able to create and sustain large markets for the low-cost mass outputs of automation. Automation requires few trained and educated people for the new kinds of jobs it does create—machine tenders and maintenance technicians in the lower ranks and scientific and mathematical experts above. Personnel (salary and wages) have tended to become capital costs—investments like so many machines. The number of workers no longer fluctuates with variations in output. Increases in product demand and hence output no longer lead to additional hiring; more people do not yield higher production. Increases in and growth of markets lead instead to management's taking greater advantage of its computers, running them longer, applying them to more functions, and installing more of them. Companies are forced to downplay the importance of training and skills. Funds are better invested elsewhere: for starters, in more smart machines.

Smarmy assurances from the apologists for automation and the trickle-down benefits of good times conveniently opacify the truths. High demand and prosperity don't of necessity favor employment. They sometimes can be seen even shrinking it, and not just over the short haul. The people in jobs can increasingly expect reduced hours at work, not in the interest of enriching leisure, but in the interest of productivity, more product for less effort, and in order to share what work there is.

If automated production is tied to expanding markets, what happens when shortages of capital, raw materials and fuels affect both consumption and production? Serious dislocations, plant shutdowns and mass layoffs, the draining of supplementary funds for the unemployed, and a drastic leveling of demand for all kinds of products and services are the results. Proposals for recovery seem not to relate to the real cause—automation, automation applied to dedicated tasks and not to the global economic system. Congress will propose emergency-related work programs for the federal government to fund at the same time that states and communities with budgets shrunk by inflation are forced to lay off thousands.

A bargain seems ready to be struck. Automation requires continued high demand and high production. Never mind that computers have obsoleted the assembly line and mass production as such, and that the customized product (Vive le Mustang!) is the child of mass specialization. Productivity and mass-marketing are still the watchwords, maximum return for minimum investment. Yet demand levels off for a stew of reasons: the maturity (!) of society and a consequent turning away from marginal goods; the shortages; high costs; environmental protection. These are some of the obdurate limitations on growth that have to be faced. Perpetual motion may be attainable as a cybernetic ideal, but perpetual growth of industrial production cannot be, not in a world that shrinks and explodes both in the same pulse. To keep the machine plugged in, therefore, the forces of production will perhaps have nothing to do but turn—the bargain, the trade-off—toward better housing, better health, education and recreation, better syntheses of the world's resources, more effective recycling. If that kind of demand can be created—which is not certain, judging from the state the railroads and cities, for instance, have been allowed to fall into—there may be growth of an inner sort to test the potential of the computer.

The unyielding, unending loop

The bargain, alas, leaves to programmable fate the lot of the disemployed. All that we've gained is continued demand and work for the computer and those who care for and feed it. Loss of jobs by attrition—no replacements hired to fill vacancies—must continue. According to Daniel Bell in *The Coming of Post-Industrial Society: A Venture in Social Forecasting*, the

> . . . new working class is to be comprised of engineers and technicians. . . . The increasing replacement of men by machines [completes] the erosion of the industrial worker. In fact, by the end of the century the proportion [of] factory workers in the labor force may be as small as the proportion of farmers today; indeed, the entire area of blue-collar work may have diminished so greatly that the term will lose its sociological meaning as new categories, more appropriate to the divisions of the new labor force, are established. . . . Instead of the industrial worker, we see the dominance of the professional and technical class in the labor force, so much so that by 1980 it will be the second largest occupational group in the society . . . and by the end of the century, the largest.

The bargain, to train the computer as a big gun of reform against social and economic ills, may also leave to chance or at best to implicit conditioning any resolution of the layers of resentment. The rhythms, not only of output, set by the computer place high demands on the waveforms of the biological system. Men and women in the superindustrial milieu are dazed a good part of the time because they seldom know what's hit them. And the fact is that usually nothing has, unless one's own ignorance may be classified a blunt instrument.

The young men at the General Motors plant in Lordstown, Ohio, in 1972 struck for twenty-one days against the mindless pace being set for them by the Unimate robots that had been put to work there on the assembly line. The incident added a term, the "Lordstown syndrome," to the language of industrial relations. It means the blue-collar blues, the alienation of the assembly-line worker. And it has the concomitant symptoms: absenteeism, listlessness, outright flaunting of work norms. Petty acts of sabotage at Lordstown included snapping ignition keys off in car locks and dropping washers into carburetors.

Nor is it far from the Lordstown syndrome to the white-collar blahs: alcoholism, expense-account and tax-return swindling, and related disorders on the management side.

There are, doubtless, as many explanations for worker disaffection and dissatisfaction as there are investigators of the phenomena. One factor that seems universal is the ambiguous nature of work. Some work because they like to; it's the exercise of an art, or it's like a game; and getting paid for it is so much gravy. Others work because it's there to do, and "someone has to do it"; getting paid for this is only right. Still others work because they need the wages to live, there's no other way; they ask for no satisfaction in the work; satisfaction comes from outside, from what they do with what they earn. Finally, probably, all three types work because they're expected to; it's what an adult must do to earn the respect of his or her elders, peers and children. It could be that simply not knowing what one wants from work, or what the driving force is, could be what alienates people from themselves and their jobs. Not knowing makes objects of them.

The labor contract

It could be too that, once one is set on a certain course, having agreed to accept the conditions, no matter how demeaning or dangerous, for a certain kind of work, the "contract" becomes inviolate. As matters are put in the transactional analysis of Eric Berne (*Games People Play*) and his successors, any change in the terms of a contract triggers an uproar. The introduction of computer work norms has to be unsettling. The worker has to feel hurt, angry, powerless or bored and so on round and round.

Investigating labor and attitudes about work in Europe, Flora Lewis of the *New York Times* found in early 1975 "a 'bloody-minded' attitude among the men and women on the production line toward output, management and the national economic situation" in Britain. A union leader told the reporter that he rejects the "Old Testament idea" of the need to work. ". . . He emphasized the need to correct injustices that society imposes on the aged, the handicapped and the poor. Reminded that Marx said not only 'to each according to his need' but also 'from each according to his ability,' he snapped, 'Marx had Old Testament ideas too!' "

In France, where the unions, even more than in Britain, are highly political, where the drive is for the workers to take over industry and to "wipe out the market economy," the centrist government tries to save the existing system "by giving labor an established role in the way management functions."

Worker participation in management is not a strange idea to the United States worker. In Sweden, the Saab experiment with team assembly units rather than lines has received considerable attention. Six workers from the major auto manufacturers returned in early 1975 after several months working at the Saab plant at Södertälje to report no particular interest in having the system imported to Michigan. The switching of tasks, which is a feature of the Swedish system, put too much pressure on the Americans, and the pace the team set for itself is faster, harder to maintain, than any efficiency system they had known at home. Participatory democracy (Toffler calls it anticipatory) is OK in Sweden; in the auto industry in the U.S. it seems several millennia away. In most American workplaces the imposed conditions are known, and, though accepted with little grace, they're preferred to any apparent confusion of roles that would result from a change. The adversary system is deeply ingrained in America, especially in the labor movement, and has its uses.

What we don't know does hurt, however. What we don't know about the computer and cybernation has to hurt if we don't move to fill in the blanks in our education. Making a reasonable, stoic adjustment to a job that one can derive no satisfaction from except outside the job is one thing; taking its permanence on faith—on the strength of formal union guarantees and, outside unions, on reasonable assurances—is another. The thrust of computerized automation and systems engineering is a total reorientation of our institutions—Alvin Toffler's "eco-spasm." What can one project concerning the automobile in five years, let alone the working conditions in Lordstown, or the quality of life in Detroit? Who's going to make the move to make it any saner?

Regardless of instinctive resistance, however, we can project, because it's already happening, as Flora Lewis found out in her interviews abroad, that work is undergoing extreme changes. We need to redefine it—and nonwork. Higher levels of retraining often exceed the capabilities of many, especially those in their forties. Only a few are able to cope with the escalating pressures to retrain, again and again, for fewer and fewer jobs. And this is only the start. There are developments now well under way that threaten to put all types of qualified men out of work—and to keep them from finding satisfactory new jobs. It is the economic purpose of automation to keep new jobs from opening. Retraining can succeed only if many new jobs are available, or won't quickly become obsolete.

Earlier assumptions, once true, become false. Earlier reasoning based upon them is no longer valid. The arguments of the 1960s about automation are deceptive. One assumption has been that more machines—not humans, but smart machines—will provide new needs for labor. Doesn't a rapid rise in the quantity of automated products create jobs? people-jobs? At lower prices, won't more people buy more clothes, homes, gadgets, God knows what? Won't more salesmen, office-workers, maintenance people and others be needed to cope with all the growing business? It's simple; whenever technical innovations are introduced, the assumption goes, more jobs are created. This is a myth. Automation creates no new jobs. New products create no new jobs. Computers do all these jobs too, very efficiently and more cheaply. It's only when office work, maintenance, sales, production and distribution require "human" labor that increased employment can be expected. Increased employment maybe, but often not for people. With the accent on productivity, the net effect need be only more jobs for more machines.

Job crises aren't just imminent; they're becoming a way of life. Our work and wage system seems ever less viable.

And the cause: self-regulating machines based on computers and feedback. They are coming to do so much of the economy's productive work that human labor of all sorts begins to command less and less income. Now a sociology or political economy to keep pace with this "subversion of work" is needed. Proposals that the government guarantee every American an adequate income as a matter of right whether he works or not take on merit. This appears to be the logical step from an economy of scarcity to one of abundance. An abrupt leap into a type of socialism is not likely to be a voting issue anytime soon, but doubts about cybernation may already foreshadow a crystallization of protest as soon as the 1976 national elections, and certainly by the 1980s. Will there be sinister plots by the middle classes to keep the poor in their place with computer-controlled special-purpose doles? Some degree of severance of income from work is obviously closer to real politics than most people now suppose.

From the beginning, the idea and the reality of Reason in the modern [industrial] period contained the elements which endangered its promise of a free and fulfilled existence: the enslavement of man by his own productivity; the glorification of delayed satisfaction; the repressive mastery of nature in man and outside; the development of human potentialities within the framework of domination. (Marcuse, *Reason and Revolution*, 1954)

The cycle can be broken. At what cost it's hard to tell. We see that automation in the end creates few jobs. We are enslaved—we as a society and not just the co-workers of the robots—by our own productivity. To maintain a level of employment sufficient to feed the American populace through wages and salaries, the system must create an ever higher demand for goods. Rules of productivity require an ever higher rate of production from an ever smaller proportion of workers, and automation continually eats away at jobs. Therefore, if income is largely from wages, the multiplication of goods far exceeds the capacity of the society to afford and consume. Earnings cannot keep up with the cost of goods. Income then must derive from something other than labor, and self-respect and fulfillment from something other than income. The productivity engine itself will come to depend on some such change in orientation.

In 1975, under pressure of the unemployment emergency, the U.S. Congress entertained proposals for federal public-service programs to provide work, according to a *New York Times* editorial, "as a matter of right for those who will remain idle after the gross national product turns upward." Reference was to a bill sponsored by congressmen Augustus Hawkins of California, Henry Reuss of Wisconsin, and eighty-five others. It set a goal of 3 percent unemployment within eighteen months. Included in the bill was a Full Employment and National Purposes Budget which would fund programs in areas like conservation, the development of resources, health care, housing, mass transit, "promotion of competitive private enterprise," and the elimination of poverty.

Public attention of this sort is some indication perhaps that a bargain with automation and the computer is not unthinkable, tentative as the beginning in a Full Employment and National Purposes Budget may be. And skirting the real issue of work and income as it does.

To repeat, computers must virtually destroy labor. They must make it obsolete, irrelevant to man's existence. And this must be turned into a brand of deliverance.

> It is safe to say that pessimism over the immediate dislocations of change will not halt technological advances, for the problems of today are clearing the way for the opportunities of tomorrow.
> (Beaumont and Helfgott in *Management, Automation and People*, 1964)

Accordingly, then, we must build more and more computers, and we must build computers that build computers. For the computer, working under man's direction—as assistant or tool or what you will—is what will produce more of the goods man wants and requires, durable, useful goods in such abundance that he himself will no longer have to toil, to waste himself, his mind and body, in order to produce and lust after them.

The vision of technological improvement, to quote Beaumont and Helfgott again,

> . . . is nothing new in the history of civilization. Man as a thinking being is also a doer—always looking to improve. Sometimes he is motivated by the economics of a situation; sometimes by an innate laziness that leads him to conceive labor-saving techniques; and sometimes by a simple urge to find a better-than-usual way of doing things.

It is possible that his existence becomes for man one of self-actualization. It's possible that men will devote their time to making themselves secure in nature, to providing the best services each is capable of, to aiding and showing love for their fellow beings. Man just might use his time for happiness, to fulfill his mind and exult in his freedom with full friendship and brotherhood. If these things are possible, man will play, among friends and with his machines. He will create and convey . . . the good things.

If all this is possible, man will have the time, the drive, the mentality to organize his life. He will understand his needs in total clarity, in some order of priority, in a continuity of self-fulfillment.

What's the use of the computer in the scheme? To find an answer, one would first have to attack the causes that slow the application of the machine to worthwhile ends, to the creation of a world of plenty, a world of fair distribution of its wonders, a world free from anxiety, fear, distrust and greed. Attack the greatest stumbling block to the exploitation of computer power and you attack the political, economic and educational managers of our civilization, those who are fighting, holding back the full use of computers. Here is the source of the timidity, near-incompetence, ignorance of human and social goals, insensitivity, that erects barriers against the democratic exploitation of computers and communications, of all technology.

New gauges of merit

People freed from want, from inequality, from the specter of public misdeeds, will welcome their new leisure as a way to find themselves as individuals, to discover their desire for happiness through creativity, love and play. But how will the good things be shared? how will they be divided? how will man measure and gauge what are his basic needs and who shall have greater shares above those needs? Men and women must learn to measure, not by inherited abilities, by geography, by ethnic accident. They must join in determining new hierarchies of value to serve as the gauges and scales of reward.

In the meantime, computers destroy labor, but they needn't destroy the laborer. Under a national, indeed a multinational, application of computers to the goals set forth in legislation, like that of Reuss and Hawkins, technology can be turned into the partner of enterprise that it was meant to be.

High-flying projections of a humane technology and a computerized utopia that serves man and industry alike are of little use amid social malaise and turmoil—eco-spasm, incipient or full-blown, call it what you will.

Off the computer in the name of King Lud

Once again, the computer stands out as a ready symbol of everything that's wrong. It is well known that previous innovations have precipitated disruptive protests. The Luddites in England in 1811–1813 were textile workers who roved in bands about the industrial north and east and smashed new labor-saving machinery in protest against reduced wages and unemployment. They took their name from a mythical Ned Lud (or Ludd), a simpleton from Leicestershire who in 1779 is supposed to have put the quietus to a stocking-making machine. "In his memory" the Luddite leaders called themselves King (or General) Lud. Between Lud and the actual Luddites in time came the inventions of Joseph-Marie Jacquard, who devised a punch-card system of thread selection in looms. This early computerization made possible the weaving of many-colored designs on one loom operated by one worker in the same time as that required for weaving plain, one-color fabrics. Jacquard's machines were in their turn violently opposed in his native Lyon. They too were seen as the cause of unemployment and actually led to the takeover of the Lyon government in 1831 by an organization of master weavers—*La Revolte des Canuts*, it was called.

Technological backlash has not duplicated in our time the proportionate disruptions of these early disorders. It is not impossible, however, that mass communications can now make a national crisis out of an otherwise local one. The bombing of the Army data center in Sterling Hall on the Madison campus of the University of Wisconsin in 1970 was only the most shocking (one bystander was killed) of a number of cases of vandalism against computers during campus unrest.

Random examples of vandalism taken from *Computer Abuse*, the Stanford Research Institute report by Donn Parker and others:

in 1968 an unknown assailant fired two shots from a pistol into a small computer at a Washington State unemployment office; damage was slight;

the computer center at Sir George Williams University (Montreal) was destroyed in 1969;

the same at Boston University the same year; wire-cutters and acid here did the damage;

students occupied the computer center on another Massachusetts campus and threatened to keep it out of operation till their demands were met;

$100,000 in damages at a chemical plant in 1970 as part of an antiwar protest; magnets were used to depolarize data;

a bombing in 1970 at the University of Kansas;

at New York University students held an Atomic Energy Commission installation for ransom;

$1 million in damage by fire-bombing at Fresno State during a student riot;

a discharged employee destroyed online files in a New Jersey computer;

a disgruntled Army officer erased purchasing data from magnetic tape; this too in 1970.

There are six cases reported for 1971. The most interesting was a penetration of a tape system belonging to a New York insurance company. Here, three computer maintenance technicians prerecorded messages and sent them by telephone to the computer. The instructions were for the machine not to rewind paper tape. This caused an endless feeding of blank tape through the read pickup. Parker's report has six cases of vandalism in 1972 and three cases through the first half of 1973. In one case an operator was finally detected by a TV monitor after two years of causing short circuits by inserting metal objects into a disk file drive; number of attempts, fifty-six; amount of damage, $500,000; motive, an overpowering urge to shut down the computer. In another case during this period, a tape librarian, having received thirty days' notice that she was fired by her insurance company employer, caused $10 million in damage by replacing magnetic tapes in the vault with new, blank ones.

Apart from the few instances of job dissatisfaction, Parker's cases of computer sabotage are not Luddite in nature. Plainly, a more generalized social protest is the motivation. Attacks on computers have high productivity in destruction to recommend them: a computer shut-down theoretically shuts down a whole organization.

Parker finds a minor incident significant—that of a Trojan Horse penetration of a shared system on a New Hampshire campus in 1973. The Trojan Horse consisted of "trapdoors" a student introduced into the file-maintenance program. When another user ran his own program, the Trojan Horse trapdoors afforded the infiltrator access at any time he chose to any of the other users' files. The break-in in this case was not malicious and no charges were brought. Parker, however, can see the technique applied in earnest and

> . . . can conceive of the vulnerability of society when it becomes dependent upon a massive network of interconnected computers. . . . Organized crime could propagate a series of hidden "trapdoors" throughout the network . . . Certain coded inputs to the system could cause selective springing of trapdoors to activate secret computer programs for transferring credit to favored accounts or extracting information detrimental to society.

Many regard a backlash against the computer—one that would take a violent form—as unlikely. There's more reason to fear a generalized groundswell of anticomputerism. The danger is not one of machine smashing. The true danger is that, out of their uncertainties, fears and doubts, people will close their minds to what good the computer, properly controlled, can do.

The Stanford study of abuses notes, bearing out the Canadian survey and others, that the computer has aroused extremely ambivalent feelings in the public at large. The computer is being hailed on the one hand as a brilliant achievement and tool to solve many of society's problems, and on the other as an "ultimate weapon" to enslave and "eventually destroy" us all. As we've said, this ambivalence may stem from the public's sense of powerlessness in the face of technology.

To what extent, Rollo May asks in *Power and Innocence: A Search for the Sources of Violence* (1972), is technology the scapegoat

> . . . and, therefore, an escape from responsibility? A student who participated in the protests at the time of the Cambodian invasion told . . . of milling around the park . . . at the moment when the protest hovered on the edge of riot. One of his fellows had shouted: "Let's get the computer!" The student then remarked to me: "All my life I've wanted to smash a computer." Now when I tell that story on my college tours the students unfailingly burst into laughter, and it is the kind of laughter that indicates that some unconscious urge in them has been released.

May sees the source of this spirit of vengeance in the students' sense of impending disaster, with technology as the smart bomb to bring it about. Unlike the primitive (or even the chimpanzee) who finds himself enlarged, extended by tools (the two sticks put together to reach the banana in the case of the primate), modern man sees technology shrinking him. In the person of the student *enragé,* he punctuates his hatred with high purpose and turns away from the very knowledge and wherewithal that could see him through the complexities he so despises.

Whether the crisis, beyond the universities and among more than the young, takes the form of outright rebellion or withdrawal (this last by severely limiting the scope of the computer in applications to social problems) will likely be determined by the character of precipitating events. However, given (1) the complexity of the computer technology, (2) the ever-accelerating pace of the computer revolution, and (3) the increasingly unstable social structure, primary determinations become important:

A. The role of computer manufacturers and users in *specifying* optimum machine and system controls as barriers to misuse.

B. The nonmachine controls, legislative and other, that may strike the necessary balances—between the right to know and the right to privacy, and between the right to use tools and the right to an income.

And maybe we're robopaths

Americans have been described as being notoriously apathetic. So viewed, they are consistently lied to, tricked, abused and misused. Their collective ire is hard to arouse. They accept dehumanization as a matter of course; their obedience is granted at will, their loyalty conferred without thought. We pay our taxes on time; we queue up in endless lines; we believe what we are told officially; we worship efficiency; and our daily requirements of emotions are received through packaged doses of TV, film and print media. Compassion, real feelings for real people who might need our help, can't be accessed seemingly because they're not summoned by an institutionalized appeal. Could it be that we are . . . robopaths?

Lewis Yablonsky in his book *Robopaths: People as Machines,* which conveys his straight-out indictment of the superindustrial wasteland, defines *robots* (from the Czech *robota,* "forced work") as machine-made simulations of people, and *robopaths* as "people whose pathology entails robotlike behavior and existence . . . human beings who have become socially dead . . . egocentric and without true compassion."

Robopaths are (1) ritualistic. The robopathic individual goes through ritualistic behavior patterns within the context of precisely defined and accepted norms and rules; his emotional behavior is programmed. Even his basic drives—

for relaxation, sex, hostility, violence—are preplanned and prepackaged. Social interactions are dull; activities, rote and trancelike.

(2) Past-oriented. Robopaths relate to what has been rather than to the situation now or to the future. Suffering from cultural lag, they respond to ideas that are no longer pertinent or functional (McLuhan's rearview mirror). It's hard for robopaths to see the future. Yablonsky suggests that the fascination with the automobile is an example of past-orientation. People are slowly dying from smog created by the internal-combustion engine, yet there is no effort to modify the system or reverse the trends that perpetuate this deadly process. The automobile and oil company executives, as robopathic as the rest, are more concerned with profits and corporate growth than with human life. And the people who buy and drive their death machines are seemingly powerless in the face of the seductive myths that invest driving a car with good sense, elan and stature. They think their latest four-wheel missile is a shot into the future when it's actually a rococo elaboration of the horseless carriage.

(3) Conforming. Robopaths have limited spontaneity and creativity. They are unable to break old patterns of behavior and to be innovative in new situations. Anyone who exhibits a manner that's in any way bizarre is feared; originality is suspect. The safest rule is to remain the same. The weirder styles of dress and hair of the sixties have become the uniform, but people who speak out in class with new and creative ideas remain pariahs to robopathic students and teachers alike. The old and sacred grooves of academe, they're the surest.

(4) Image-involved. The robopath is David Riesman's other-directed man. What he considers appropriate is derived from what an image of status dictates. Those around the robopath lay down the rules, not an inner radar based on principles of conduct. Fashion rules.

(5) Acompassionate. If compassion entails a true con-

cern for the interests of others, at times at one's own expense, robopaths lack compassion. They are neither for nor against other people in terms of a personal moral attachment. They act when they believe acting is expedient, a boost to their status or image in society. According to Yablonsky, they have no humanistic values that structure their behavior. Neither compassionate nor noncompassionate by choice or denial, they are simply deficient in fellow-feeling, acompassionate, without social conscience. Yet their consciences are clear. Examples of acompassionate robopaths are the "good German" who "stonewalled" in the face of evidence of the death camps; economists who think more of protecting farm income than of feeding the famine victims of the sub-Sahara; the profiteers in Medicare- and Medicaid-financed homes for the aged. Another word for acompassionate is pusillanimous: taking care of yourself and doing no more than you have to for anyone else.

(6) Hostile. People unable to act out of their spontaneous and creative natures develop repressed, venomous pockets of hostility. They have a gratuitous sense of rightness in denying free expression, in saying no, in punishing the unrepressed, and in seeing anyone who enjoys himself made to pay *their* price. Bureaucrats have an acceptable structure that allows them to vent their hostility on other people: "the rules don't permit . . ." or "we regret that we can't comply . . ." Homicidal outbursts by otherwise calm and structured people, like Charles Whitman, who killed fifteen and injured thirty-four from the tower at the University of Texas, are bloodier forms of the same venting process. Another way the average robopath can act out his enormous hostility is to elect candidates who espouse "law and order," "all-out victory," "keeping the so-and-sos in their place," and "capital punishment."

(7) Self-righteous. The robopathic are narrow-minded superconformists. They are never deviant, as they look at things, or against the social machine. What they do is right

as opposed to the sinfulness or laxity of everyone else. Theirs is a hard case: conforming to rules they accuse everyone else of slighting. Because of his eternal "rightness," the robopath is seldom disturbed by guilt or anxiety. He has his own finely tuned access to the social will and conscience. Adolph Eichmann (a classic robopathic "hero") was most self-righteous about carrying out and defending his executive part in the "final solution." Lieutenant Calley's routine killings of "Oriental civilians" were marvelously self-righteous; even more so was his unflappable defense. Marvelous too was the mass affirmation he received from a robopathic majority and its president. (One poll revealed that 75 percent of the population disapproved of his conviction.) Robopathic parents inflict a repressive, inflexible discipline on their children to make them conform, all by conviction, self-righteous conviction. In effect they build their children into robopathic people in their own image.

(8) Alienated. The robopathic person appears to be "together," but in actuality he is alienated from himself, from others and from the natural environment. Robopaths are components of a social machine. They are alienated from other people because they interact with others as objects, not as human beings; they occupy roles, as children, students, employees, other bodies on a bus or plane, other objects in the anonymous crowd. There is no room for compassion. Compassion toward objects would be *crazy*.

Robopathy, according to Yablonsky, is a ". . . complex phenomenon. It's a condition that can afflict people of all ages and in all [parts] of society. Some roles . . . are more prone to [robopathy] than others, and some societies have more robopathic roles than others." Oriented to a machine-directed technology, emotions have become too cheap, too plentiful; they're simply not "in" anymore. Emotions come spewing out of millions of TV sets, movies, the arts, newspapers, books and magazines ad nauseam. To some, it's not unlikely that we'll soon accept the concept of "disposable citizens": those too old, too ill or too infirm to be socially, economically or politically useful. Indicative are the cases of forced sterilization.

Yablonsky's correctives are awareness, the spontaneous counterculture, and strategies for innovation. The difficult task of piercing the self-righteous armor of the robopath would seem to make of education in awareness a slim hope. The dropouts from the social machine offer some hope, again slim, of sustaining islands of humanity. And institutions such as Synanon and practices like psychodrama (recommended by Yablonsky) afford media for attaining self-awareness, the foremost hiatus in the makeup of the robopath. But the appeals here, as with the countercultures, are limited. Work goes on with the machine, and it doesn't have to be robopathic.

Rollo May gives us a Chinese parable, first cited by Werner Heisenberg, which cautions that dedication to the machine makes us tend to act

> in a machine-like manner. Whoever does his business in the manner of a machine develops a machine heart. Whoever has a machine heart in his breast loses his simplicity. Whoever loses his simplicity becomes uncertain in the impulses of his spirit. Uncertainty in the impulses of the spirit is something that is incompatible with truth.

The question of the horse and its rider

With the acceptance among the nonrobopaths, the non-dropouts—in short, you and me—of the inevitability of accelerating change, the important plan seems to be balance: no one cure-all, no wide-eyed trust in the computer, but some reasonable expectation that with a massive dose of knowledge and respect for "the impulses of the spirit," some order may be put into the electronic course of events.

On the place of the individual, Rollo May points out that

> . . . practically no one remembers the names of the astronauts who walked on the moon. What we do remember is the machinery; the hero of the moon trip was not an individual but a projectile, and the men were tenders of this projectile [and of its onboard and backup computers].
>
> Let no one conclude from this, however, that in the new age man will be subordinate to technology. It may be just the opposite: the development of technology, filling a role similar to that of the ancient slaves, may force us to find intellectual and spiritual content to fill the vacuum of our days and nights.

The battle with robopathy might be lost, however, before the great day, before the electronic helots set us free from bodily and mental tedium. "We all learn," Toffler observes, "from our environment, scanning it constantly—though perhaps unconsciously—for models to emulate. These models are not only people. They are, increasingly, machines. By their presence, we are subtly conditioned to think along certain lines."

> Recently [Toffler continues], the computer has touched off a storm of fresh ideas about man as an interacting part of larger systems, about his physiology, the way he learns, the way he remembers, the way he makes decisions. Virtually every intellectual discipline from political science to family psychology has been hit by a wave of imaginative hypotheses triggered by the invention and diffusion of the computer . . .

If the clock gave us the fragmented cause-and-effect concept of existence, what will the computer's virtual negation of the need to think and calculate on time and in series do to man's orientation? Serial, time-bound relationships will have to be observed, but this can be left to the machine. Time-bound, late second-millennium man, verging on the third, might well shudder and dose up on something when he takes a good look at all the promised nights and days of Socratic bliss.

And there'll be work to do—if only to keep safe our rights to vacuous nightmares. As fighting wars can't be left to the military, so, we'll doubtless learn, data processing can't be left to the technocrats. Toffler again:

> He [the technocrat] fails to recognize that the faster pace of change demands—and creates—a new kind of information system in society: a loop, rather than a ladder [—thinking in top-to-bottom terms without provision for feedback]. Information must pulse through this loop at accelerating speeds, with the output of one group becoming the input for many others, so that no group, however politically potent it may seem, can independently set goals for the whole.
>
> As the number of social components multiplies, and change jolts and destabilizes the entire system, the power of subgroups to wreak havoc on the whole is tremendously amplified.
>
> To master change we shall . . . need both a clarification of important long-range social goals *and* a democratization of the way in which we arrive at them . . . a breathtaking affirmation of popular democracy.
>
> The time has come for a dramatic reassessment of the directions of change, a reassessment made not by the politicians or the sociologists or the clergy or the elitist revolutionaries, not by technicians or college presidents, but by the people themselves. We need, quite literally, to "go to the people" with a question that is almost never asked of them: "What kind of a world do you want ten, twenty, or thirty years from now?" We need to initiate, in short, a continuing plebiscite on the future.

Never mind practical questions on the validity of popular expressions of opinion through polls and letters and calls to the White House, Congress and the local paper. Electronic information-gathering and polling can hardly be more reliable than traditional means, and it may even be more subject to tampering. Still, Toffler's anticipatory democracy, however implemented, touches a receptive nerve in a society confused and abused by meritless authorities. Such high-flying proposals can't be too far removed from the animating purpose behind the down-to-earth-and-statistics Reuss-Hawkins Full Employment and National Purposes Bill.

As pointed out by James Martin and Adrian R. D. Norman in *The Computerized Society*, 1970, if we were to discontinue hardware development and concentrate on implementation, we'd "spend the next fifty years learning how to program and use today's machines and building up data banks for them . . ." But the reverse has been the case. Development goes into firmware—software incorporated into hardware—and the miniaturization still to come will fuel this continuing impulse. As Herman H. Goldstine, a pioneer with von Neumann, writes:

> . . . the whole point of great increases in speed is to handle totally novel situations not possible before. Once one can predict the weather 24 hours in advance in a quarter of an hour, it is not worth a great deal to be able to cut this to one second, but it would be worth enormous amounts if one could predict the weather for 30 days in advance in a quarter of an hour.

Implementing the hardware that's already here is too expensive, even with the plummeting costs of microprocessors, for some transactions. Getting two-way terminals into 100 million homes still calls for some severe cost-cutting, especially for the "banking" of the information that would make any widespread dialogue (Mr. Machine meet Mr. and Ms. John Q. . . .) meaningful.

We're not, as Martin and Norman observe, witnessing a computer explosion. Explosions die away after the fallout. Computerization and advances in automation and cybernetics show no signs of dying away, with a bang or a whimper. They carry the force of their own perpetuation, for good or bad or both.

To some, and they might be the smart ones, robopaths or not, information technology is clearly too powerful to control, and one's only chance for survival may be *shucking,* simply to tell *them* what *they* want to hear. Still, in Vincent

Canby's words in another connection, "the primacy of man when man's given half the chance" is not to be denied. Man will go with the computer, on whatever lovely ride, or the computer won't go at all. It's not a horse that can survive without the rider.

chapter 00011

The Technological Marriage of Logic and Arithmetic

In the first two chapters we examined the intellectual impact of computers and the double effect of the machine, for good and ill, in matters of privacy and employment, touching only tangentially on the technology. We shall now investigate the technology, mathematics, economics and other associated aspects of computers, their history, their function, their capabilities and, ultimately, whom they benefit.

Productivity is the name of the game.

Productivity is the raison d'être of business, industry and multinational corporations bent on reaping bigger and bigger returns, and an essential part of the drive for productivity is the computer—from the giant mainframes that handle input from a number of attached and remote terminals to the naked minis fixed to an appliance, a machine or instrument for sensing, decoding and processing events and signals.

From the outset, productivity has been the spoken goal or unintended result in every advance of computer technology. The substitution of vacuum tubes for relays increased the speed and power of the machines and turned them from straightforward, efficient calculators into the first true computers. Speed and power weren't the only gains. Nor are leaps in processing capacity now from nano- to picosecond speeds the only benefits from continued research into micrologic and microstorage. As a primary example, in the early days, interchangeable control panels or circuit boards, cards or paper tapes contained the programmed instructions. Detailed instructions had to be wired in or read into the machine as the work progressed. No one set out to make the computer operate on its own, though that was the thrust and the outcome. To the early developers it seemed something had to be done to reduce the error-susceptible physical intervention of the operator.

Enter John von Neumann in 1944 and his *First Draft*, setting forth the logical functions of computations, and from this the concept of incorporating stored programming in EDVAC and in the computers to come. And so it has been ever since. At any stage of development of the art, efforts at wiring programs into the system, incorporating them, have led to more autonomy for the machines. The needs of the processing unit for instructions as it works out a problem are anticipated, and the machine is enabled to address its own storage of instructions in much the same way as it addresses its bank of information. "It could even be made to modify its own instructions as dictated by developing stages of work" (IBM Student Text). This is what designs evolving from von Neumann's ideas accomplished in the forties, and it's what microprocessing, microcomputers, MOS (metal-oxide semiconductor) chips accomplish today . . . what developments in bubble, laser and holograph techniques will continue to strive for in the foreseeable future.

So much for progress. . . . What's behind it?

As is often the case, outside economic factors work as a catalyst for the development of technology. In recent times, inflation provided the expanded earnings and from them the increased capital to invite more and more companies into the cycle of producing goods both for industry and for the consumer. Incessant pressures on corporations for growth at any cost have pushed and pulled business executives into modernization, more and more computerization for greater "peopleless" efficiency. The results have been endless production, stringent automation in both plant and office, relentless expansion of machine-controlled marketing and distribution. Inflation also expanded purchasing power, multiplying the needs and desires for more and more products, faster and more convenient services. Always in company with inflation come continually spiraling prices and consumer complaints. The executive suite turns these complaints against the rising cost of labor, never against the rising cost of profits.

Large computer units sell for upwards of $8 million and rent for as much as $200,000 a month. For a small company, say a manufacturer with sales under $25 million a year, an advanced computer at a rental of $10,000 to $25,000 a month can handle payroll, market analyses and any number of other administrative functions, and more than pay for itself in the salaries (labor) it saves and in the timeliness and quality of the information it generates. A company of this size may well use as many as ten computers—two or three large ones and several minis or megaminis. Minicomputers, up to $10,000 in cost; and megaminis, up to $50,000, are machines designed largely for special functions, such as the monitoring of a mixing process where parameters of quantity, heat and pressure have to be controlled. This is not to say that minis and especially megaminis cannot handle large general-purpose information-processing tasks as well. The dividing lines are not impassable barriers, just as they aren't, on the lower end of the scale, between the smaller minis and the microcomputers.

The prices here are meant only to indicate general ranges; each installation calls for distinctive attachments or peripherals appropriate to the job to be done. A firm or organization goes through elaborate studies to determine what kind of computer to buy or rent, and what modifications of the basic design might be needed. The job to be done has to be no greater than and is ideally and most often far below the capacity of the equipment selected. It is said that, as in the human brain, only 5 percent of a computer's capacity is put to use.

Roughly, the ratio of purchase price to monthly rental is fifty to one, and the expected "life" of an installation is five years. Before the five years are up, the user is likely to expand and update his installation as new technology comes "on stream" and as he realizes the projected benefits. He's likely to budget from ½ to 2 percent of his annual sales to computers. One survey—of the paper industry—indicates that from $50 to $750 goes into all the costs of EDP for every employee on a company's payroll. The average and the median are both somewhat more than $200 per employee among the companies surveyed.

More people will use computers when the individual user has to know less about their inner workings in order to make them function. The more the arcana of programming are put into the chips and mainframes, the more time the user can put into digesting the data and exercising his decision-making prerogatives—"to substitute brass for brains," in Lord Kelvin's words (brass in the machines, that is, to free the brain from the drudgery of calculation). Low salaries and high profits are more the means than the end; what corporate energies really go into, in computer marketing, in oil, in paper, in banking, are those ever-vanishing saturation points in a technological market. The more potential there is in a market, the greater the chance for the individual firm with the technology to get in early and dominate. Witness Xerox in copying and duplicating, IBM in computers.

And, parenthetically, watch now the fearsome jockeying for the right start into two-way television. Two-way TV is the home computer linked to data banks and processing by way of cable TV, bringing the computer to the homemaker. How computer technology is applied will have everything to do with how this potentially very rich market will be exploited. Perhaps partial efforts on a "dedicated" footing will be the way home terminals come to saturate the nationwide market. Tocom, Inc., of Texas, for instance, serves the Rossmoor Leisure World Community in Arizona with a combination of entertainment, security checks on residences, and medical communications. The capability for interaction between home and computer is there; it simply awaits implementation, the right crossing of supply and demand. IDR System, a service of Reuters, Ltd., the worldwide newswire company, furnishes one-way computer access by cable. The system can become two-way as the market grows, and it may extend from financial information, as at present, to racing results, a large market, and eventually into homes with a broad coverage of general news. Home Box Office, Inc., a subsidiary of Time, Inc., has made moves toward a nationwide satellite network of pay-TV systems.

The push of technology is there, but gigantic systems and institutions are there too, like the press and TV, and they can't readily abandon the known for the unknown. Putting the daily newspaper onto home terminals, with the possibility of selective printouts, has to be a fairly scary prospect for those already making a go of the "old" ways. The technology exists, for instance, for storing microfilm pages of the *New York Times* in the *Times* Information Bank, and yet the Bank uses a platoon or more of editors, abstracters and indexers in addition to the paper's regular news personnel. In one way of looking at it, the *Times* does its work twice, for these abstracters go over the daily editions of their own paper as well as fifty-nine other publications in preparing the material for the Information Bank. If the Bank used microfilm facsimiles, and beyond that holography, it would be, as they say, home free. But the Bank is a going unit on a limited technological footing. Romantic and futuristic giant steps can't just be taken without some care to present methods and staff conditions. The latest electric typewriter, such as Xerox's Daisy for another example, could be a third the present size, but marketing dictates the bulk and "solidity" of IBM's Selectric, the stylesetter of them all. The first typewriters in the 1880s looked like sewing machines. The typewriter of the future will likely be nothing but a holder for paper attached to a microphone or a TouchTone keyboard, or both in deluxe versions—the keyboard being for times when dictation would be too noisy.

Predictions, culture lag and future shock, however, are grist for other mills. Technology, here, every day in every way, is mystery enough. A mystery which is baffling for the layman to understand, yet all too real in technological results.

Technology, for example, has produced the microcomputer, the simplest, smallest and densest computer made in amount of processing per cubic measure. It can be as small as a solid-state integrated circuit (IC) device, or chip, of about $\frac{1}{8}'' \times \frac{1}{8}''$—the size, as most books on the subject say, of the capital O in this type face. Most often chips are part of the arrayed circuitry of larger packages and systems, but, strictly speaking, they are by themselves computers. Depending on architecture (how it's made), an IC can contain a microscopic network of processing and storage elements with interfaces or connections to input and output. With from ten to a hundred cells or components mounted or applied to its surface, or contained within it, the IC is called a medium-scale integrated circuit (MSI), and with more than one hundred, it's called a large-scale integrated circuit (LSI). These are fine distinctions, but the terms, like so many others, appear relentlessly, and it's good, maybe, to have the distinctions spelled out in one place.

What the circuits do essentially, no matter their size, is to carry miniaturization one exponential step down (or up in density) from the transistor, which in itself is a miniature of the vacuum tube. Not only is the IC a miniature transistor, but also it's a miniature arrangement of transistors—bipolar circuits, diodes and transistors of many types. (Rein Turn lists seventeen LSIs in an effort to classify this complex new species.) The point seems to be not miniaturization for its own sake, but miniaturization for the sake of higher productivity: more for the same or less, as in Goldstine's example of the thirty-day weather forecast done in the same time it takes to do one day.

There seems no stopping place either in the look backwards or in the look into the future. As already stated, the vacuum tube was the condensed alternative to the relay switch in the early days. Without the vacuum tube there'd have been no computer as we know it, or computer revolution. Succinctly, according to Goldstine,

> . . . there are two time factors which enter into the total reaction time of a circuit involving a relay or vacuum tube. First, there is a time required to actuate the relay or tube, and, second, a time to actuate the resistors, capacitors, and inductors making up the remainder of the circuit.
>
> In the case of a relay it takes anywhere from 1 to 10 milliseconds . . . to cause a relay physically to open or close. This time is due to the inertia of the mechanical parts, and it is in the nature of macroscopic things that most mechanical motions do take times in the millisecond, or longer, time scale. In the case of a vacuum tube—or of a transistor—all motion is at the microscopic level. The elements being moved are electrons, and they have

> masses of 9×10^{-28} grams [that's 27 zeros and then "9" to the right of a decimal point] as compared to relay contacts whose masses are usually about 1 gram. Thus there is essentially no inertia to be overcome, and a vacuum tube [or a transistor or an IC] can be said to operate almost instantaneously for our purposes.
>
> The time required to actuate the other parts of a circuit, e.g., to charge the capacitors, is determined by the value of the resistances, capacitances, and inductances. It can be made very small. In the case of the ENIAC [Electronic Numerical Integrator and Computer, the forerunner to EDVAC, page nineteen] this time was on the order of 5 microseconds. . . . Thus the electronic technique is at least a thousand times faster than the electromechanical [or relay technique]. In fact, at the present time (1971) electronic circuits can be made to operate in nanoseconds—billionths of a second. This is the reason why the first and most primitive electronic computer . . . was several hundred times faster than the best of the relay machines.

The vaporized interconnection (integration) of microscopic resistors, capacitors and inductors is the fantastic, but logical, extension of those early decisions.

As one proceeds, the names in the technical lexicon start overlapping—transistors, semiconductors, chips, MOS (pronounced "moss") chips—and they slip into everyday English, certainly in the business pages of the newspaper and in the trade journals, without a great deal of care being taken as to precise meanings. In any case, the transistor is the granddaddy of all these microscopic wizardries. Perfected at Bell Labs in the early fifties, the transistor was the first great leap into miniaturization, following upon the move from relays to tubes as described by Goldstine. Essentially, a transistor consists of a semiconductor block, or resistor, and an arrangement of electrodes, depending on the function—whether induction, capacitance or resistance. The name *semiconductor*, which has been applied to a whole class of microcircuits, derives from the property of the chemical element it's made from (mostly silicon but also germanium; both are ceramic). The semiconductor has an electrical conductivity that at normal temperature is intermediate between that of a metal and an insulator. Semiconductor devices are greatly utilized in circuits requiring "on" and "off" or "high" and "low" states. Again, two states are required for computing circuits.

By the use of these properties on a microscopic scale, logic states are set down on a chip in multiples. One chip, by the architecture of its elements or cells, may carry an elaborate set of instructions or storage data. It can be made to execute the additions, multiplications and so forth of a single instrument like the calculator or a washing machine, or it can be combined on mainframes or other larger computer units to perform or store discrete functions.

To appreciate the importance of the semiconductors, we have to take a look at what they have replaced in a number of configurations: ferrite cores. Inside a medium- or large-size computer, these are tiny ringlike or doughnut-shaped devices that are strung at the intersections of a grid of wires. The grids are held on frames, and the frames are layered in stacks. The current in the wires maintains the cores at a given state of polarization—+ or −, 0 or 1, etc. By the change of current in any given wire—to put the matter simply, and there are variances—the magnetization of a given core can be changed from positive to negative, and vice versa. At one or another state, the ferrite core is a bit of information, a given, a datum. And minute as they are, ferrite cores are four times less dense than conductors, and their speeds are less by at least one order of magnitude (1:10, 10:100, 100:10,000, etc.). Comparisons are crude and elusive because of the dynamic nature of the technologies. Ferrite cores and other magnetic devices (as opposed to intrinsically electronic units like semiconductors) will continue to be used but largely in the central storage and processing areas. Semiconductors, because their manufacture can be more extensively automated than cores and because of density and speed, will dominate, however.

What's more, they are modular, plug-inable, and adaptable to a range of applications.

In a semiconductor chip, the circuit elements, the gates and cells of the microprocessor, are the oxidized, photographically exposed areas on the ceramic base or substrate. In manufacturing, the major costs are for "makeready"—design and artwork. Depending on the complexity, this can amount to from $10,000 to $100,000. Obviously the low costs per unit, which make thirty-dollar calculators possible, result from the number of usable chips you can make from the basic design and stages of processing.

A single chip will be designed for certain logic or storage functions, and these will necessitate a given array of transistors and interconnecting (integrating) paths. The design of the single chip will relate to how it is to be arranged with other chips in a "package." The package will contain as many chips as it has I/O pins. These pins are for wiring or inserting or both to mainframe or to whatever other larger unit the package is intended to serve. The trick is to come up with the best combination of functions within a chip—the lowest cost for the fastest and most reliable possible operation—and beyond that, the best combination of chips within a package.

From the design comes the artwork, which is a laying out of masks on a magnified scale. The masks are then reduced photographically to final chip size, and these are stepped-and-repeated to produce a number of copies or replicates for laying down on one wafer of ceramic. A typical wafer is 2" in diameter, and it will contain from 200 to 400 chips. The imposed masks expose the areas of the base to oxidation, diffusion, crystallization, film deposits, and a number of other physical and chemical processes in a sequence of stages, these interspersed with cleaning, photosensitizing, photo-exposing and etching. Rigorous testing of each chip on a wafer follows each stage. The number of rejects is sizeable—from 25 to 50 percent.

With an overall batch cost of $100,000 and a yield of barely 250 good chips from a run, it's plain that a single chip will cost about $400. Chips can cost far less, though: under $25 apiece, say. The selling price will of course depend on market—how many to a single buyer and through what selling channels.

Because of the variety of uses they're put to, it's impossible to state, with any precision, how much computation or execution a single chip is capable of. A MOS containing 1,024 memory cells could theoretically allow access to 60 million bits of information a second, on the basis of a read/write (retrieval) time of 16 nanoseconds or 16-billionths of a second (16×10^{-9}).

Miniaturization, it's obvious, doesn't begin and end with semiconductors. Wire gauges and core diameters will be reduced, and therefore magnetic storage will also gain in density and speed, though an irreducible minimum of wire thickness seems to limit core to reductions up to a point that is far short of standard MOS densities, let alone what can be expected from ongoing research. Beyond these two are a number of other technologies which in one way or another strengthen the trend toward higher productivity. The most promising seem to be cylindrical domain and electro-optical techniques. In the former classification are domain tips and bubbles; in the latter, many adaptations of lasers to the inducing of logic states as well as to the production of holographs—the ultimate in miniaturized reproduction of information. The technology in all cases is extremely complex, and factors such as heat and stability have much to do with any eventual adoption of them for workable systems.

The mighty bits of electronic computation

Any layman who has had a glimpse of a printed circuit board is doubtless fascinated by this marvelous new "geography." Reds, blues, yellows, greens—all lead this way and that; here and there blobs of colored epoxy, connectors and blocks, bugs and towers—an out-of-scale juxtaposing of unrelated objects, a surrealist urban landscape that seems to make its own inevitable sense. Maybe too he is turned off by a terrain he's convinced he never could, nor even want to, master.

In many ways, electronic circuitry and the computer it powers may be easier to understand, for all the complexity, than automobiles and airplanes. The boards and other circuits are, in simplest terms, devices for "making sense" of the magnetic states of the electric cells that comprise them.

A magnetic state is either plus or minus, oriented north or south, clockwise or counterclockwise. Current through the units of an IC board, of a ferrite core stack, or of any other like array finds the units "on" or "off," depending on their state of magnetization. These on or off states are data, and data constitute information when they take on meaning. The first level of meaning the computer achieves is the distinction between the two mutually exclusive states. The quality of information is its quantity—that is, how much information is contained in a message that consists of plus or minus magnetic units.

The computer system marries logic and arithmetic. It takes numbering back to a time when man counted without fingers (not in multiples of ten, decimally, but by singles or pairs of units). There are many mathematical roots, and routes, to mechanical and electronic calculation, but perhaps the most interesting and most fruitful is that through symbolic logic and specifically through the system of Boolean algebra. George Boole (1815–1864) conceived an algebra for logical statements and notation that was the same as traditional algebra with one startling exception. To Boole, $x^2 = x$. Boolean symbols or signs, in Goldstine's explanation, stand for "things or groups or classes."

What about the operations of + and · ? [he goes on] Consider first the latter, · . If x stands for "black things" and y for "cows," then $x \cdot y$ or xy stands for "black cows." In general, xy represents that thing having both properties x and y. Thus if x stands for "horned things," y for "cows," and z for "black things," then xyz stands for "horned, black cows." Now if both x and y are the same thing—say, "cows"—then xy expresses no more than x. In other words

$$x^2 = xx = x,$$

which is Boole's special law that sets logic apart from ordinary algebra.

The + "is used to relate totally disparate things and . . . to collect them together into a new thing or class," so that $z(x + y)$, standing singly for Americans (men and women), comes together to form the new class of "American men and women." And inversely there is the operation of separating the whole into parts, so that $z = x - y$, with the signs representing planets, stars, and suns, forms the proposition: "stars, except the planets, are suns." Goldstine proceeds:

Boole had a very clear idea of the relation of his logical system to algebra. He said: "Let us conceive, then, of an Algebra in which the symbols x, y, z, &c. admit indifferently of the values 0 and 1, and of these values alone. The laws, the axioms, and the processes of such an Algebra will be identical in their whole extent with the laws, the axioms, and the processes of an Algebra of Logic. Difference of interpretation will alone divide them. Upon this principle the method of the following work is established." The reason for 0, 1, of course, is that these are the only quantities satisfying the equation $x^2 = x$.

(One times one, or one square, is one; zero times zero, or zero square, is zero.) In logic, what this becomes to Boole is that " 'the symbols 0 and 1 . . . are *Nothing* and *Universe.*' "

It took some doing to get from Boole into the binary logic and arithmetic of machine computations. Even ENIAC, the first electronic computer, trading relays for tubes, operated in decimal. The implications of binary logic did not occur to the pioneers except when EDVAC came into consideration as a cost-saving and more efficient machine—fewer tubes—than its forebear. In a sense, binary arithmetic would have been too costly for ENIAC. The machine already had 17,000 tubes, and binary might have required almost four times that many. However, with the introduction of mercury delay lines into EDVAC, the new machine could store 1,000 binary digits at a cost of 10 tubes—a 100-times savings, and binary became the "medicine of choice" for the new machine.

In binary arithmetic, there is no single-digit designation for quantities of more than 1. Two is 10 (01 + 01); three is 10 + 01 = 11; 11 + 01 = 100 (4 in decimal). A table for decimal 0 to 16 with binary equivalents follows:

decimal	*binary*	*decimal*	*binary*
0	00000	9	01001
1	00001	10	01010
2	00010	11	01011
3	00011	12	01100
4	00100	13	01101
5	00101	14	01110
6	00110	15	01111
7	00111	16	10000
8	01000		

It soon becomes obvious that, in length alone, binary is awkward. Indeed, binary numbering, beyond 9, takes as many as three and a half times the digits to represent a numerical value as does decimal. For instance, 99 is 1100011 in binary (that's 7 digits in binary to 2 in decimal, 3.5×).

In each set of oppositions, as with binary versus decimal, we're dealing with trade-offs or an exchange of benefits. The "awkwardness" of binary, for example, is more than made up for in the speed of the electronic pathways, by the aptness of the Boolean polarities, and by the innate simplicity: no tables of addition or multiplication to store.

These characteristics of binary and the trade-offs are related more to understanding the operations of the machines than to actually being able to use them. In any case, the concept of place values is fundamental. The place value indicates the value of the base number raised to the power of the position of a digit reading from right to left, so that the first four place values for base 10, decimal, are as follows:

Position/power of 10	3	2	1	0
Place value	1,000	100	10	1

Using this table, 165 decimal, for example, is seen to have 1 hundred (1×10^2) + 6 tens (6×10^1) + 5 units (5×10^0). In binary (carried to six positions):

Position/power of 2	5	4	3	2	1	0
Place value	32	16	8	4	2	1
Binary representation	100000	10000	1000	100	10	1

Such a table can be extended leftward to infinity. Position 6 has a place value of 64 and produces binary 1000000.

Besides binary there are several other mathematical concepts with a bearing on machine efficiency and design. They include: whether serial or parallel addition is to be performed, and whether floating-point or fixed-point arithmetic. Another basic alternative, more grammatical than mathematical, is fixed or variable word-length. Machines are designed to add either in series or in parallel. Serial addition is the way we're taught from childhood—pre–New Math childhood, anyway—one pair of digits at a time. We do

$$\begin{array}{r} 75 \\ +18 \\ \hline 93 \end{array}$$

as 5 and 8 is 13, put down 3 and carry 1; 1 carried and 1 is 2 and 7 is 9, put down 9; the answer is 93. In binary, serial addition looks like

```
   111    (7)
 + 111    (7)
   ---
    10
   10
  10
  ----
  1110    (14)
```

The adder in the processing unit in the machine matches each pair in turn from position 0 leftward and totalizes the results of each operation. In parallel addition, the two sets of digits are matched at once:

```
  111
  111
  ---
  000    Sums
 111     Carries
 ----
 1110    Final sum
```

The serial operation is slower, but it takes less hardware. One processing unit handles each of the paired additions in turn: three steps in the example here. In parallel, each factor to be added is treated as a word, and the words are combined in one step, the unit of execution being of necessity a more complex array of adders.

ENIAC worked decimals in parallel; EDVAC, binary in serial. Von Neumann and Goldstine considered this shift one of the principal improvements in design, and for many years serial was the preferred technique. Now, however, with the increased density brought to hardware by the microcircuits, the additional hardware can be supported in the interest of speed. Parallel addition is extended, too, to the whole concept of processing: many elements of a program, as well as programs from satellite systems, are handled in parallel rather than in series, in queues or schedules.

Machines are designed to do either fixed- or floating-point arithmetic. Till recently, floating point was achieved only through software. The machine operated on a fixed-point basis, and the user had to keep track of his decimal (or binary) point through complex sets of instructions. A computer hardwired (adjusted or designed) for floating point normalizes the point as numbers are entered into the machine. As operations are carried out, the points float to the right or left, the computer seeking to get all the numbers involved in the calculation into the same power (of two or ten, as the case may be). It's like reducing fractions in ordinary arithmetic to the lowest common denominator. The process is called *scaling.* To the computer circuits all numbers, whether whole numbers (integers) to the left of the point, or fractions to the right, are the same. Scaling brings the positions of operands into line for correct addition, subtraction, multiplication and division. The essential difference between a fixed-point and a floating-point computer is that in the former the operator has to perform the scaling, and in the latter the machine does it for him. Operating on one LSI chip, modern pocket calculators function as floating-point systems.

It goes without saying that for a machine to be able to carry out operations that make sense, the strings of bits entered into the machine must make sense. The higher-level languages—Fortran, Cobol, and others—as well as machine-recognizable inputs carry new data and instructions, and these inputs must conform to how the machines are built to handle them. In a fixed-word-length computer, bits are stored in strings to form words of a predetermined length—24, 32, 36, 48, 64. Data in memory are coded to fit this standard. Each word may carry several first bits as an address (location of particular item of information). And when these address bits are part of any given instruction, the whole word, of 32 bits, say, is brought out of storage as a unit and the execution proceeds. In variable-word-length operations, data are not confined to these standard lengths, and bits or bytes (ordinarily 4- or 8-bit units carrying parts of a word) can be stored at separate addresses. It's as if the word *definition* were in the dictionary not as one word in one location, but in four locations, one for each of its syllables. To extract the whole word for processing, the instructions would have to carry the starting location—say, for *def*—and a coding for the number of syllables (bytes) in order to indicate word termination. The succeeding syllables would then be brought out in order following *def,* and the fourth syllable *tion* would be counted as the end of the word. The trade-offs between fixed- and variable-length designs are complex. Variable tends to cut down on storage hardware, but it necessitates either complex programming or firmware. Fixed-length is essentially faster, because words can be fetched and operated on in parallel, but it limits coding to the standard units. Microprocessing is enabling words of greater length to be built in, even in the smaller (aerospace and other "traveling") systems, as well as a wider use of variable (byte-oriented) lengths with a consequent boost in flexibility.

These barest glimmers perhaps suggest the limitless possibilities of the computer using binary and all the consequent codes. Thirty-two binary cells offer 4 billion plus (4,294,967,296—2^{32}) combinations of 0s and 1s. What's the world's population? If there's a code beyond simple numbering that would distinguish each inhabitant within one coded word of 32 bits, one addressable MOS chip could run through an identified list of the world's population in less than two seconds.

To handle this in the real world in the computer with its array of powerful cores and chips, the user or programmer has just to sit down and go to work. His or hers is the job of putting in the intelligence. The more the programmer inserts in the way of self-correcting routines, the more the computer is being pushed to full capacity. This is so no matter how much intelligence is wired in.

There are "evaluating" programs designed to compare results and so to reach decisions. If a result is, for example, a certain quantity or less, the computer might be made to "order" a machine turned on or an airplane to move to another altitude. Light and dark spots in TV projections can also be made to serve as binary input, and arrangements of them can be made to generate pictures, graphs, maps and even musical compositions, or better yet maybe, *jets d'eau,* fireworks, and lightshow accompaniments to musical compositions.

The program codes cause the instructions to be executed, and they also orchestrate the work of all the peripherals. The program fetches words from punched cards (on which the binary code is a function of the perforations), paper tape, magnetic tape, disk and drum storage. The fetch can take the form of queries on a terminal printer or CRT display, in which case the programmer or user is expected to supply the needed answer. Through telephone, coaxial cable, microwave or satellite communications, or through any combination of these, the terminal can be anywhere from across the room to the near side of Jupiter. Compilers within the machines allow for the translation and decoding of machine language into and out of natural or program language.

The usual descriptive division of the computer is into five interacting parts. The *input* is both the forms the data take, the media that contain them (punched cards and so forth), and the machines or components that perform the entering of the data. The *central processing unit* (CPU) is the part of the system that handles the instructions, interprets and executes them. It's also called the mainframe. *Control* contains the programs that supervise the routines of the CPU; it handles the routing of data in and out and does other housekeeping routines, as well as microprogramming that may be added to suit the special needs of the installation. A typical element of control hardware is a read-only memory (ROM, rhymes with Tom) semiconductor chip. It contains an array of instructions which the CPU and other functions access under certain conditions. Ordinarily a ROM is fixed; it can't be changed: instruction words are read but not erased (or, if erased, then the magnetization returned to the state it was in before the read was executed). Still there are some ROMs that can be modified. Other parts of control are basic-, tape-, and disk-operating systems. These too can be either ROM chips or core elements that are not meant to be modified.

Storage is the collectivity of memory units, which may be separate from or integral with any other part of the system. As a distinct entity it's usually called primary storage or main memory, the depository of data that are to be most immediately acted upon.

Memories or storage functions are described according to a number of factors: their properties or methods of working; what they're made of, their location, application or function. So there is volatile storage (vulnerable to loss during power cutoffs), permanent or fixed storage (read-only or non-erasable), dynamic (movable according to program and not always available for recovery), and static (not dynamic, available), to name but a few. Storage or memory can be kept on any of the recording materials, such as punchcards and magnetic tape, and be made available to the CPU. Tape and cards can be accessed only serially. A stack of cards or a reel or cassette of tape must be searched in order to retrieve any information it's known to contain. Other storage means, disks, drums, the MOS chips and the experimental bubble and laser techniques, provide direct and instant random access by address to any bit, byte or word, wherever located in the system. The point here is that with RAM (random access memory), data may be brought into operation without having to run through a whole series of unwanted data first. Main memory, subject to the control function and on call by the CPU, may contain both permanent and temporary storage. Data in temporary will typically be shunting, as needed by the program, between main and secondary or offline storage.

The capacity of an operating system is expressed in terms of the thousands (Ks) or millions (Ms) of units of data that main storage can hold. We get readings of 32K (32,000) or 16M (16,000,000), which mean that the machine or component in question has the space for storing 32,000 units or 16 million, as the case may be. What's in the unit—whether a bit, a character (symbol of variable length), a byte or a word—has to be known for the K or M to have significance.

The *output* division of a computer is both the form of data and the devices and channels that process the executed information for use outside the operating system. Many of the devices and channels are both input and output; hence *I/O* as a designation for all equipment and data involved in communicating with the computer. It's maybe worth observing that here the computer is less specialized than man. Unlike the eyes and ears, which have receiving functions only, the CRT and keyboard send as well as receive information.

The microprocessor as microcomputer, that tiny "urban landscape," contains all these functions. A chip or configuration of chips in a package does all the work—on a lesser scale—of the larger systems. The pins in a package are the I/O terminals; other components do the processing, controlling, storing.

If this is so, then why the larger systems? Why minicomputers if there are micros, and why large systems if there are megaminis and minis that can do the job? The question seems to answer itself, for the distinctions are matters of scale. And putting the smallest, most productive unit to work is the objective—whether alone or in arrays with other units of the same size or not. The largest systems can be so many "micros" (in scale at least) when sixty-four of them are combined in one massive array, as is the case with ILLIAC IV, probably one of the most powerful systems in operation. The big systems haven't the look of dinosaurs yet; they'll only get bigger, indications are, as the micros get more microscopic.

The family tree

Microcomputers and microprocessors do not a fourth generation make. Though some think they do, they are more likely part of the third generation of computers—an advancement, it's true, of some magnitude, through miniaturization that began with IC boards in the mid-sixties.

"Geological" time for computers is after all no more than three decades. To be sure, there were the "prehistoric" and pioneering efforts before 1945. There was, for example, Ramon Lull's Ars magna device in the thirteenth century with which he set about to confound infidels. His rotating, inscribed wheels were intended to prove the existence of God. There were others: the arithmetical machines of Blaise Pascal and Gottfried Wilhelm Leibniz in the seventeenth century; the Earl of Stanhope's generator of the eighteenth; the Jacquard punchcard loom; the difference engines of Charles Babbage and Pehr Georg Scheutz, Lord Kelvin's tide predictor, the harmonic analyzer of Albert A. Michelson and Samuel W. Stratton, the logic machines by William Stanley Jevons and Allan Marquand, all in the nineteenth century, as well as the fast pace of corollary inventions from the telegraph, the telephone and the switchboard, through the early, workable Hollerith sorting and counting punchcards (from which came the birth of IBM), the typewriter and Othmar Mergenthaler's leap into near automation with the linotype; railroad switching control; to motion pictures, radio and television. In the 1930s came the differential analyzer based on designs of Vannevar Bush and his colleagues at MIT. Within the decade that included World War II the Harvard–IBM (electromechanical relay) Mark I was developed; ENIAC and EDVAC at the Moore School of Engineering of the University of Pennsylvania, too; as well as the IAS (for the Institute for Advanced Study, at Princeton) computer—those principally, but others under development in the United States and abroad constitute the important early work. The list of theorists and inventors include, in addition to von Neumann and Goldstine: John V. Atanasoff, Howard H. Aiken and Clair D. Lake, J. Presper Eckert and John W. Mauchley, George Stibitz and Claude Shannon. For comprehensive history of the technology, the mathematics and logic, Herman Goldstine's *The Computer: From Pascal to von Neumann* is recommended. The author's measured enthusiasm for his own participation in the frontier days of computerization is catching—well worth the journey through what hard theory there has to be in any such account.

The first, second and third generations of the computer are usually distinguished according to the density of memory and the type of circuitry:

Generation 1 (to 1958): vacuum tubes; 1 million characters of memory to 400 cubic feet; $1.26 per 100,000 multiplications. Typical systems were UNIVAC I and IBM series 700.

Generation 2 (to 1967): transistors and the beginnings of solid-state components; 1 million characters to 100 cubic feet; $0.26 per 100,000 multiplications; IBM 7090, Philco 2000, CDC (Control Data) 6600, Burroughs 5500, IBM 360, and the supercomputers, UNIVAC's LARC and IBM's STRETCH.

Generation 3 (to present): integrated circuits, MSI and

LSI, a growing trend toward multiprocessing, the development of minicomputers and microprocessors. One million characters per cubic foot and less; $0.01 per 100,000 multiplications; IBM 370/158 and 168; Burroughs 6500 and 7700; ILLIAC IV; Honeywell 66 and 68; as well as MULTICS; UNIVAC's 1110, 1100/20 and 40; Goodyear Aerospace STARAN; CDC STAR-100; the U.S. Navy's AADC (All Applications Digital Computer).

To many, IBM among them, and Rein Turn of the Rand Corporation, the fourth generation is upon us and has been since the introduction in 1972 of the IBM 370/168. This incorporates MOS and a great deal of inter-system processing and communications hookups. It's not accepted unanimously as a single, true departure from the third generation, however. Too many of the new developments are simply refinements of those immediately preceding.

And what of the future? Personal, portable, hand-carried, or next-to-the-tube microcomputers as terminals will surely bring about great changes inside and outside the industry. There are portable terminals that come with a keyboard fitted with a two-color ribbon. Users type their instructions in one color, and the computer offers answers in another. The materials worked with or developed during a session with a specific problem are retained. Nothing is lost when the plug or jack is pulled out or the switch is thrown. Everything can be resumed at a later time.

Not only the terminals but other intelligent peripherals contain the microprocessors that can very cheaply emulate the complex operations formerly confined to the mainframes. No longer are expensive hardwired, single-purpose circuitry and mainframe power required. Input, whether from humans at keyboards or from sensor machines and other "slave" units, can be filtered, checked, compressed, "buffered," and otherwise digested before it passes by local telephone to the larger transmitting systems, like long-lines, microwave, and cable. Output can be "branched" to meet the needs of the user, whether man or machine. Time, space and distance take on new meanings. With access to the constellation of new think ports, the mainframes divide their time through parallel processing, yet lose no capacity for any of the individual users. No one term—multiprocessing, resource-sharing, concurrent execution of virtual or transparent machines—seems adequate to describe this fourth-dimensional reach of the late third generation. New definitions arise seemingly with each new installation.

Firmware in the form of ROM chips and structured programming takes on great importance. Software—the set of programs, procedures, compilers, library routines, manuals, circuit diagrams—has a history of lagging behind hardware. In the early days most program sections were handmade and unique to the system. And since then, manufacturers have allowed software and hardware to play something like a game of leapfrog. A new operating system will surpass the heft of existing software. Within several years the software will then leap beyond the capacity of the system and so set the stage for the next major change in equipment. By the time that's on the market, present software will prove deficient, and the process goes on.

Structured programming is a philosophy of software design that has a very strong technical base. It enables the design, coding and modular testing of large projects. Maintenance and documentation are simplified. Huge data bases and banking programs like electronic funds transfer (EFTS) are made that much more feasible as a result. Programming is becoming engineering instead of black magic, which has not infrequently been its mystique.

The program banks of users, manufacturers and EDP service firms furnish a stockpile of subsystems to add to a system's basic software. It all adds up—the smart terminals and minisystems, the firmware and user-directed software—to the wave of the future, the multiple installation of whatever size. Whether running minicomputers singly, in tandem, or in batteries along with stacked micros and full-size federations of mainframes linked by all available communications, the single console or terminal opens a great new world to the users. It gets what they call low-cost guaranteed uptime, faster and more accurate response, and far easier file access. Even within the third generation such resources have been a luxury.

Communications interlace the computer world. New common carriers and equipment marketers are cutting into the dominance of AT&T in this field. The prize: lower costs to the users, and more users. Transmission rates based on volume rather than distance, and other user-to-user conveniences are in the offing. Information is no longer anchored to huge batch machines. It has become a readily available and instant-access commodity. "The advantages of systems using remote terminals," Rein Turn observes, "are overwhelming compared to the old 'batch processing' systems where decks of [punchcards] had to be left at the computer room for subsequent processing and pickup, with turnaround time as long as 24 hours."

Online, long-distance processing will do more to cut down commuter and freeway traffic jams than improved trains, buses and roads ever could. Personal contact in business may not go out entirely, but it must certainly change, as will the office as a place that one has to man—and woman—nine to five. Home terminals, briefcase black boxes, pay stations everywhere could make a computer your home wherever you hang your hat and plug in.

I/O peripherals, containing the phenomenal microprocessors, are of several types. First are the hard-copy devices: card readers and punches, optical-character readers (OCRs), line- and page-printers and graphic plotters. These are ordinarily linked to the operating system through tape and disk storage. Next, the interactive, two-way terminals, which come equipped with keyboard and typewriter-printer, graphic displays and some voice processing systems. Last, there are one-way entry devices with either keyboards, or voice and character recognition, or sensing transducers—these last, noninteractive and limited to data-gathering.

Big (not big at all) brothers to the hand calculator are several types of hand-held I/O terminals. One available model, made by Termiflex of Concord, Massachusetts, the size of a shaving kit, contains 1,000 characters of memory that can be called up and displayed alphanumerically. There is a twenty-place keyboard for inputting data or for programming the master operating system. Transmission can be by teletypewriter or (attached to an acoustic coupler) by telephone. The system also plugs directly on site into larger systems.

In many ways, "the terminal's the thing." As the marketing of home terminals materializes, as the consumer encounters more and more point-of-sale units in stores and service centers of all kinds, as the controls of cars on dashboards become more and more computer-oriented, the smart terminal is likely to replace the great whirring giants with the flickering lights as the public's idea of the computer. And, indeed, the impression won't be far off the mark, for with fuller development of the microdevices, the terminal will take on a large share of specialized processing work.

In 1973 there were 200,000 online data terminals installed. There should be 2.5 million of them by 1980, if just present uses continue and expand to exploit new multiprocessing developments. What level this will reach, if just a portion of the home-terminal potential is realized, is impossible to predict.

A quiet revolution

Technology, of course, doesn't come charging in always on a flying horse and clear away everything old in its path. The new makes its way with the old. For example, the introduction of electronics into telephone switching: a quiet revolution. It's well known that AT&T is no stranger to electronics and computers; it developed the transistor, and has contributed since to semiconductor research.

Electronics in phone service has many roles. Electronic switching systems (ESS) deliver the most pervasive impact. At the heart of ESS is the microprocessor. As part of a variety of packages, the microdevices replace traditional panel and crossbar relay systems. The new circuits are "under the direction of a pair of [large] computers that watch over each other like Roman consuls, or like the 'redundant' computers of an Apollo lunar landing craft."

Electronic systems, as a *New York Times* article of April 6, 1975 (by Victor K. McElheny), so well puts it, are "racing a moving target." The old systems cannot be scrapped outright. For one thing, they undergo technological improvement themselves; for another, they are providing the services they're supposed to. Innovation for its own sake is a luxury that few, even Ma Bell, can afford or justify.

> The introduction of a new switching system isn't a matter to be taken lightly [McElheny quotes one Bell official]. Vast amounts of capital are required, the system must live for many years in an ever-changing environment and it must work compatibly with the existing electromechanical plant . . .

So with ITT in its operations abroad and serving institutional intercom accounts, with AT&T, and with the 1,700 independent telephone companies throughout the United States, as well as countless others abroad, electronic switching is phased into existing systems, not imposed as a replacement.

What the consumer will know or knows already of this "quiet revolution" will be numerous "glamor features" like conferencing as well as the ability to reach operators or emergency numbers from pay phones without depositing a coin and the automatic interception of calls to nonworking numbers. This last service is variously known as Voice Answer-Back (VAB) and Automatic Intercept System (AIS). AIS delivers a message that's made up from stored segments of a recorded human voice, like:

The number you have reached
In the
Is not in service
Please check the number
. . . etc.

The coherent message comes out, as everyone has by now heard, something like:

The number you have reached, 36811-hundred, is not in service in the 201 area. Please check the number and dial again. If you need assistance, please stay on the line and an operator will answer.

The memory consists of two ninety-six-track magnetic drums, again the duplicate Roman consuls for reliability. The central processor of the system works on timing pulses to change the connections from one word or phrase to the next. (There's a set of spoken digits from 0 to 9 with a neutral inflection and a set with a falling inflection, for the ends of sentences.) The central processor also has a store of unassigned, "nonworking," numbers in all the central offices served by the intercept system. A single file will consist of a 46-bit word: the 7-digit number, its status (changed, disconnected or whatever), and a count of calls to the number (to serve as guidance as to when to reassign the number). If the party has been assigned a new number in an area served by the system, the drum will include that, and the processor can include it in an announcement such as:

The number you have reached
Has been changed.
The new number is . . .

If no new number is stored or no other pertinent message can be assembled automatically, the call is then routed to an operator who, working with a CRT, will have a printout of the situation as it stands and from that hopefully can give the customer what he needs to complete his call.

More totally electronic than anything Bell has announced for wide public service are ITT's several electronic exchange systems for private users. Handling upwards of 100 extensions, ITT's electronic switching chops the caller's voice by means of a pulsing circuit at a rate of 16,000 samples per voice per second. The system "polls" all the extensions in the exchange at this rapid rate and processes them digitally and in sequence on a single main line. All the receivers in the exchange receive the chopped samples in proper order, and the phone dialed receives only those samples it's supposed to receive, and without distortion.

The telephone instrument becomes an interactive terminal when it has access, as it has in the General Electric Information Service, to a voice synthesizer like Votrax. Developed by Richard T. Gagnon and manufactured under license by Federal Screw Works, Votrax translates 8-bit computer codes (or bytes) into voice particles (phonemes). Eight bits afford, as we've seen, 256 combinations (from 00000000 to 11111111). In Votrax any of these bytes is made to signify any one of four inflections of 63 different speech sounds (252 sounds in all)—enough to generate an unlimited vocabulary, 300,000 words in the GE system.

General Electric's Mark III allows its subscribers to call Votrax and to enter data into the computer directly over the phone. The computer voice requests an identification number that is known only to authorized users. The user taps in his ID on a standard twelve-key TouchTone instrument, and the session with the computer proceeds. (Standard rotary dialing can be used too if the mouthpiece is fitted with an inexpensive device for generating the beeps.) Everything entered is verified—spoken back to the user by the synthesized computer voice to make sure there's been no error in transmission. Votrax may also, according to program, request further data and give answers that result from the processing in the computer. A typical session with the service (GE calls it TIP, for "telephone information processing") will cost from twenty-five cents to a dollar per minute—the difference depending on the complexity of the computer work being done.

Anyone concerned with the manipulation of words—in writing, editing, translating, teaching languages, speaking, reading—might easily see the endless utility of Votrax. The interest now will be in seeing how it is made to reach the right consumer.

Some uncommon electronic sense for the driver

Electronic systems for cars have been projected for close to a decade, and expectations of revolutionary changes have fallen far short. Ignition, fuel injection, braking, general performance, lighting, transmission, radio and tape player, voltage regulator, seatbelt interlock, all received boosts in effectiveness and efficiency from transistors and solid-state devices, but a central use of microprocessing for overall control remains far from realization. The tempo, however, is picking up.

In February 1975, President Ford said at a news conference that the auto makers had given him a written promise of a 40 percent improvement in fuel consumption within five years. Proposals of ways to accomplish this multiplied, and with them the complexity of the problem became clear. There were the add-ons from outside the auto industry and more elaborate central controls from within. RCA, Rockwell International, and other giants with a strong lead in microprocessing came forward in the spring of 1975 with a series of innovations. Chrysler became the first of the auto makers to step forward with a "radically modified computerized engine that does away with the catalytic converter and improves fuel consumption." Two computers are designed for the task, each a white box 10" x $3\frac{1}{4}$" x $2\frac{1}{2}$" mounted under the hood. They are meant to process data from the position of the accelerator pedal and from temperature readings of the outside air and of the coolant, and then to order the firing of individual spark plugs at the instant calculated both to minimize the emission of pollutants and to maximize fuel economy. The promise to the President of 40 percent economy was, RCA claimed, within reach of fulfillment by electronic devices; Chrysler was more restrained—5 to 10 percent was all it held out for its white-box twins.

The auto makers generally have been less than promiscuous in their embrace of microprocessor ideas from outside their own research.

> The fanciest microprocessor or computer [a Chrysler spokesman was reported by Richard Witkin of the *New York Times* to have said in April 1975] was only one element of the desired system. . . . The trick . . . is to be able to gather the inputs for the computer from the car's mechanical systems and then to perfect the anatomical devices—distributors, carburetors, chokes and the like—that could accept instructions from the computer. . . . The maximum improvement in fuel consumption over current cars that could be expected simply from electronic controls was 15 percent. . . . The rest of the 40 percent improvement . . . promised President Ford . . . is expected to come from design of lighter-weight cars and from the increased role of compacts in the total mix of cars sold.

Plainly, Detroit was as uncomfortable with technological

pressure from other industries as it has been with governmental or Nader-like dictations of standards. Plainly too, the history of fuel management in jet aviation indicates that substantial increases in gas savings, as much as 100 to 150 percent, are achievable. It remains to be said that easy solutions don't deliver the definitive answers. Many technologies have to be brought together. For instance, the people who make the microprocessors are not the same as those who make the sensors—thermocouples, pressure transducers—that are necessary to supply the readings that an onboard computer is meant to process. Spokesmen for semiconductor firms in 1975 were not optimistic. Onboard computers to handle all the inputs that govern performance weren't expected to be standard in cars till at least the early 1980s, they said.

There have been ideas for automating the whole process of driving a car. Proposals include zeroing devices on the highway that would regulate steering and speed by way of solid-state interactions between cars and roadway implacements. There has been interesting research into an accident-prevention radar that works off sensitized license plates. This is an RCA system, which, in addition to the special reactive plate, involves (1) a solid-state antenna for locating a car in relation to the car ahead, and (2) interrogating sensors that can be positioned in police patrol cars, on the side of the road or imbedded in traffic lanes. The practical effects would be to warn a driver by signal that he's going too fast, or too fast for hazardous conditions; to cause the brakes to be automatically applied to avoid rear-end collisions; to warn a driver when he's going the wrong way in a one-way street; to identify stolen cars for the police; to monitor vehicles for possible safety infractions; to serve as a call for ambulances and service trucks in cases of emergency; and to act as a kind of BART system at toll booths to allow drivers with a payment or credit arrangement to be billed rather than to have to stop to pay tolls.

(BART, as we know, stands for Bay Area Rapid Transit, the San Francisco subway system which incorporates many computer installations, not the least of them a "money card" or magnetized commutation ticket. This wallet-size plastic card provides a line of credit against its owner's purchase price. Each time it is used to gain entry to a BART platform or train, the cost of a ride is deducted electronically from the owner's entitlement and so recorded on the magnetic card. When he runs out of entitlement, he pays in cash for a particular ride or buys a new card.)

Computers in everyday life

Point-of-sale terminals become the most obvious place for everyday encounters with the computer. An installation might be in a gas service station. There, with the pumps linked to a minicomputer, the customer inserts money or a credit card into a terminal and is OK'd or not for self-service; how much less the gas will be, no one is saying. A card can be checked for credit standing. If the account is delinquent, a printout to this effect is triggered; if the card is stolen, the machine is programmed to keep it. On money transactions or when the card is OK, the terminal allows the pump to deliver the amount paid for or ordered, and no more; OK'd credit accounts are billed.

This, like the EFTS (electronic funds transfer system) connection of supermarket to bank to customer, will be one of the many variations tried before several systems win out as the most acceptable. There are the systems involving the thick and thin bar codes that have for several years been appearing in one form or another on railroad cars, truck trailers, and merchandise; there are recognition systems that scan products holographically and compare the image with a stored program that then outputs price and other information to the cash register terminal.

Bar codes on labels can be read by a scanner port in a checkout counter or by a light pen attached by cord to a register. The code used for items in a supermarket is a simple configuration of parallel lines and spaces that gives a full range of alphanumeric coding. A number or character consists, in standard systems, of four lines and three spaces—seven bits of information in all. Lines as well as spaces are either wide or narrow, thick or thin. The wide bit is more than twice the width of a narrow one.

By mid-1975 about half the products in supermarkets carried the universal product code, but only several handfuls of stores out of 50,000 in the nation were conducting experiments with it. The checkout station using the system includes a window set in the counter surface. Packages passed over it expose the bar code to an optical scanner, which transmits the information to a minicomputer—either part of the cash register, or separate—as a central processor for a number of registers. The minicomputer causes the register to enter the sale on the tape that is run for each customer. The system is obviously faster than normal checkouts. Consequently the number of clerks can be reduced. There is even speculation that scanning can be applied to a self-service, cheatproof procedure, and this would further cut down on personnel costs. Beyond direct savings are the informational by-products: each transaction becomes part of an online inventory of goods in stock, on order and in need of ordering; the record constitutes a built-in customer-preference survey.

Retail stores—Sears, Montgomery Ward, Macy's, J. C. Penney and others of that sort—have gone more heavily into point-of-sale (POS) equipment than have the supermarkets. Their system uses light pens or wands to read one version or another of the universal product code that has been printed on the tags and labels of merchandise. The companies dominating the field are Singer, NCR, and IBM. Numbers of installations that are reliable or meaningful are hard to come by, but the general feeling is that the market potential is tremendous. No one talks of the possible adverse effect on employment, for as things stand the salesperson in the variety or specialty store will remain an important "POS device" himself. Installations of this type of equipment will only make him more productive, it's hoped —cutting out the salescheck and the daily balancing of sales book against cash drawer—and will give the store a far more timely and comprehensive grasp of what's going on in its movement of goods and cash.

There are many systems of bank automation—money cards, "communicated" checkless deposits of wages and salary, automatic tellers, each being one form or another of electronic funds transfer systems (EFTS). Each such innovation ties banking, in unforeseen ways, into many phases of everyday life and necessitates some redefinitions of banking practice. The supermarket terminal that hooks up to a savings bank brings the savings bank or other loan institution into commercial banking. No matter the kind of institution that works out an EFTS arrangement with a number of stores, however, it soon becomes obvious that additional online control of the clearance of funds becomes a real need.

Banking and insurance companies are surely among the most experienced and most sophisticated users of electronic information. Yet the proliferation of services has transported the banks to unexplored shores, and their efforts to meet the new possibilities and demands seem to leave them, in cybernetic terms, hunting. In New York, four of the principal banks were said in April 1975 to be developing a prototype of a common switching system that they might use to funnel funds-transfer data between retailers and their respective banks.

Bankers in Utah succeeded in early 1975 in having their state senate pass legislation to put a moratorium till July 1976 on any EFTS installations. The principal fear, according to *Computerworld* (March 19, 1975), was that out-of-state banks would otherwise set up terminals and thereby establish branches without first "asking for a charter." The United States Controller of the Currency, who regulates national banks, had placed a moratorium too on the placing of remote terminals anywhere beyond a fifty-mile radius of an established branch.

Under consideration by the Federal Reserve Board and the Federal Deposit Insurance Corporation, in April 1975, was the extension to savings banks of the right to conduct preauthorized transactions. Preauthorization allows a bank to pay a customer's bills without a check, to transfer funds, as a matter of monthly agreement or upon notification by phone. This is but another blurring of the line between checking and savings accounts.

The *New York Times* (April 8, 1975) quotes an urban affairs specialist:

> The effects of electronic funds transfer will be drastic, but it's impossible to say now exactly what they will be. Obviously, there will be destabilizing effects on employment in financial institutions and retailing and possibly other fields, and in the real estate market. And the whole way that people do business may have to change, because they will be deprived of the "float" that's now built into the system of paper transfers of funds.

Furthermore, the *Times* writer goes on, the banks "which now have the free use of many millions of dollars daily could lose much of this lucrative reservoir of funds when money is transferred instantly with electronics." As if there weren't enough juggling of options already, several retailers have bought savings and loan companies and thereby taken on the combined role of merchant and banker.

Before weeping over the plight of Mr. Chase and Mr. Manhattan, one might down a comp-u-martini at the nearest electro-alcoholic dispensary and turn his attention to the workings of automated crime-busting. The Safe-Streets Act of 1968 established the Law Enforcement Assistance Administration, and this body has in the period since dispensed upwards of $4 billion to police and criminal justice systems on the federal, state, and community levels.

Perhaps a quarter of the funds went to improving communications, according to Nicholas M. Horrock in the *Times*,

> to reduce what the police call "response time," the period between the report of a crime and the arrival of officers. The assumption was that arrests could be sharply increased and crime deterred by swift police action. The response time of the police in many departments has been cut, but the incidence of crime has not.

On a single day, according to IBM in 1972, the computer at the National Crime Information Center (NCIC), which operates under FBI direction and is tied directly into more than eighty police departments and indirectly into many more, handles upwards of 60,000 inquiries.

A true story, with names changed, etc., illustrates the way the system is capable of working on the patrol-car level. Two Idaho state troopers chase a speeding car. Before they stop the offender they radio his out-of-state license number to headquarters. There the dispatcher enters the number into his keyboard terminal, which transmits the message to NCIC in Washington, D.C. NCIC queries its computer file of stolen vehicles and finds the car is indeed stolen. Idaho is so notified, and the dispatcher, within seconds of having received the call from the patrol car, radios back: "Bring him in; the plates are stolen." The offender, originally only wanted for speeding, turns out to be a dangerous fugitive from a California arrest with a Missouri car stolen in Alabama. Without the NCIC network of computer and communications, the man probably would have got off with a ticket for speeding.

IBM, in its *Computers Are Going to Town* (1972), describes a metropolitan network, New York City's SPRINT.

When a citizen calls the police emergency number 911, it is received by one of 52 police operators, who process complaints through display terminals connected to the central computer. The computer contains a list of all city addresses and the current location and status of every patrol car in the city (each patrol car assigned to an incident reports in every half hour to update the computer information).

The computer automatically verifies the address and reports the incident to one of 18 radio dispatchers who [are in] direct radio communication with the patrol cars closest to the scene and lists the name of the nearest hospital. It also alerts police personnel by special routing to the need for special equipment, such as an ambulance, and reports the occurrence of unusual events that must be reported to other city departments immediately.

When a patrol car is assigned to a call, the computer automatically records the time. If the patrolmen do not report in half an hour, the SPRINT system alerts the radio dispatcher to check into the situation and take appropriate action—for example, sending another car to investigate.

In addition to speeding response to emergency calls, the system gives each dispatcher a continuous record of the disposition of all patrol cars under his control. This simplifies the dispatching of cars, permitting less experienced personnel to handle the job effectively and shortening the training time for new dispatchers.

Putting two-way terminals in patrol cars is an easy-to-visualize broadening of the network. In an installation under test in the San Francisco Bay Area, to run a check on a suspicious car without uttering a word, a patrolman need only tap the letters and numbers of the license plate on the keyboard that's mounted on the transmission hump of his cruiser's front seat. The terminal's microcomputer processes the request and passes it along to the control network. (One computer facility serves nine counties in the San Francisco–Oakland area.) Control, which is in instant communication with both the state and NCIC networks, responds within six to sixty seconds and displays on the small screen attached to the keyboard information the patrolman needs to dispose of his inquiry.

Stolen cars aren't the only concern of law enforcement, but they do serve seemingly as a major vehicle in the travels of criminals. License numbers, stolen or not, like Social Security numbers, are unique identifiers, and a system for tracking the movement of wanted (or unwanted?) people by way of the cars they use has proved productive.

To design a tracking system for a nation like Canada, according to Elliot Nestle of Interdata, Inc., a maker of minicomputers, involves starting with the specifications for a realistic network and then going through a step-by-step selection of equipment and lines. The goal is the immediate retrieval and update of database files. The system must allow an officer access through a terminal to a central file in his investigation of suspicious cars and drivers. The central computer too has to be able to send out reports of summonses issued and other police information relating to cars, either to a given terminal, to all the terminals in a region, or to all the terminals in the system.

In actuality, some 1,500 terminals will be needed, some in remote locations and some in cities. Most will be in police stations, some in the homes of officers who work a lot on their own, and some in police cars. The terminals must operate under extreme conditions—extreme hot and cold, humidity, vibration, and dust—they must be the same throughout the country, and they must cost less than $1,000 each.

The terminals tend to form clusters in which all are within fifty miles of each other. But clusters may be hundreds and perhaps thousands of miles apart. The farthest point may be from three to four thousand miles from the database at the central site. The traffic from each terminal is low, about one message every ten minutes, or no more than 10 percent of capacity each day. The officer will key in an inquiry of from forty to sixty characters, and the computer will answer with a message of from 300 to 1,000 characters—a ratio of computer output to terminal input of about five to one. The response must appear within six seconds, and the terminal must produce hard copy, since the officer may have to carry the message during an investigation and since the response has to stand as an official record. The traffic reaching the database from all the terminals will arrive at a rate of about forty messages a second. About 25 percent of the messages will be rejected by the host computer because of errors in keyboarding or errors that occur in the transmission lines. In addition, because the system is to operate twenty-four hours a day and because there's a three-hour time differential across the nation, the ratio of peak to minimum traffic will be no greater than five to one—a very small ratio compared with those of 100 : 1 which often pertain in more localized networks.

Reliability and availability must be nearly total. Momentary delays or short busy signals can be tolerated as long as, during a delay, the control will let the officer know that he is still connected, perhaps by periodically printing BUSY till the computer is ready to process his inquiry. Finally, the database and the transmission network must be secure enough to prevent unauthorized persons from obtaining information they're not entitled to, by law or otherwise, and the network must be low-cost, either readily available from the telephone system or easy to set up from scratch.

The configuration that results from this Canadian study includes a combination of trade-offs: a pair of redundant minicomputers with redundant front-end processors (for controlling transmissions in and out) rather than one large system—redundancy for the obvious fail-soft advantages; remote data-concentrators and multiplexers for "ganging" the transmissions from the terminals; a combination of low-speed telegraphic and high-speed private telephone lines to gain the lowest cost and the highest level of security against malicious or accidental infiltration; an electronic keyboard with nonimpact, thermal printer; and access by contention rather than polling, because contention is more suitable to the more complex but cheaper telecommunications selected.

It becomes obvious that computer networks do not reduce crime, but they can make the on-the-line officer more productive, and when the dollars for hardware are carefully budgeted, they can produce a system that's not all gimmickry. We'll now see that much the same rationale applies to the uses of computers in medicine.

Some electronic choices in medicine

Computers, solid-state instruments, closed-circuit, two-way monitoring, diagnosis and therapy will not, cannot, wipe out disease and death. However, care and prevention can gain, as they usually have, from reasoned, systematic approaches to the hitherto unknown.

A "laundry list" shows how wide and many-branched are the effects of electronics, communications and data processing in health care: lung-function testing, microsurgery, apparatus for ventilating patients and assisting their breathing; computer-aided diagnosis, imaging equipment—X rays, ultrasonic- and laser-scanning; electronic microscopes; the digitizing and transmission of images for remote diagnosis and referral, computer-assisted measurements such as electrocardiography; biofeedback; intensive-care units for adults and with adaptations to the miniaturized parameters of fetuses and the newborn; nuclear medicine and the control of therapeutic and diagnostic radioisotopes —the list may be endless; it's surely a subject for a book in itself.

RCA's Videovoice is one example. The terminal combines a TV camera, a CRT monitor, a two-way speaker-microphone, and facilities for tape-recording image and voice. Over telephone lines, physicians are able to consult instantaneously on X rays, electrocardiograms (ECG), and electroencephalograms (EEG), as well as charts and records. Closeups are possible for detailed inspection. Plainly, devices like Videovoice have "conferencing" applications outside medicine. Businessmen and technicians can come together electronically for discussions of charts, printed copy, visualizations of parts, components and products.

Industrial Research reported in its February 1972 issue on computer-aided diagnosis:

> . . . a group at the University of Missouri Medical Center has developed a computer program that can diagnose a type of heart disease from x-ray pictures more accurately than a team of specialists. The . . . type involved . . . rheumatic heart . . . affects the . . . valves and disturbs the flow of blood through the heart. As a result, the shape of the heart is slightly distorted. In fact, there [are several] types, and the actual distortion depends on what [particular ailment] the patient is suffering.

The Missouri team, headed by Dr. Gwilym S. Lodwick, designed the computer program to spot the distortions in heart X rays. The program measures the exact light intensity of each point on the film and uses these intensities to sketch the actual shape of the heart. The computer then compares the sketch with shapes stored in its memory—actual X rays of patients with different forms of rheumatic heart and X rays of disease-free subjects. This matching produces the diagnosis of the X ray in question. Again from *Industrial Research:*

To test the program's diagnostic ability, Lodwick put himself and nine other radiologists in direct competition with it. The object of the exercise was to diagnose some 300 heart x-rays from a library of cases. The computer achieved an overall accuracy of 73% in diagnosing the presence and type of rheumatic heart disease; the radiologists, 62%.

Indeed, no individual radiologist performed as well as the computer. And while regarding the test as very much a preliminary study, the Missouri radiologists foresee the computer's use in many other areas of radiology, including the interpretation of mass-screening x-rays.

Straightforward information handling, we've seen, has a lot to do with health care (1) in the recordkeeping in hospitals, in clinics and in private practice; (2) in the maintenance of peer review organizations (PSRO); and (3) in the handling and assessment of programs and regulations by local, state and national bureaus. All of these functions tie together: the individual doctor's files and more, those of the hospital, become part of the public records, and they in turn affect in countless ways how medical care is taught, paid for, dispensed and sometimes improved.

The bulk of the flow of information begins in a hospital with the admissions questionnaire, and it goes all the way through the patient's stay, entering into the system, manually or by computer, every detail. The handling of much if not all of this information is grist for the EDP mill.

Two-way terminals in wards, for instance, can give the staff instant access to case histories and to records of medication as well as a means to enter new information, not for their own purpose alone but also for billing, purchasing, scheduling treatment and whatever else. No reasonable person fears that medical people will be automated out of their livelihoods. It's rather easy, in fact, to picture benefits all around if in no other way than in cutting down, as EDP almost must do, on the nonmedical donkey work of the profession. Health costs are rising, and the ratio of physicians to patients struggles to keep pace with the rise in the general population and in its demand for ever more sophisticated medical attention.

There are, however, built-in problems: the relationship between doctor and patient is special, surely one of mankind's oldest, and one of those most laden with trust as well as misgiving. The sanctity and frailty of information having to do with health are uppermost in the minds of both parties to the medical contract. You might be bursting to show the scars of your own operation; you just don't want someone else doing it for you. More important, one of the worst things a doctor or nurse can have at hand, needless to say, is the wrong information. For these and other reasons, medical files are guarded and subject to overlays upon overlays of professional, legal and moral constraints. The suggestion of computerization and the possibilities that raises of unauthorized access are virtual red capes to those in medicine. The sharpness of the issue is nowhere more obvious than in the rising incidence of malpractice suits and in the profession's sensitivity to its own exposure to attack—much of this grounded on the patient's right to know.

In *Datamation* (April 1970), as cited by the excellent annotated bibliography in the MIT portion of *Data Security*, Dr. F. R. Gabrielli calls attention to the inevitable pressures for the release of medical information: pressure from employers, credit agencies, police or private investigators.

> Would the databank administrator be sufficiently independent to withstand such pressures? Legal justice and scientific progress frequently demand use of medical data at the expense of personal privacy. In some states, private communication between the patient and doctor is not considered privileged in court. Until these problems are solved, it is difficult to try to build a basis for privacy in massive databanks.

One of the most elaborate data processing systems in medicine is that of the Kaiser Permanente Care Program in California. There, the use of multiphasic screening has been under development for some time, and there, according to IBM,

> a computer has been programmed to analyze automated tests for blood chemistry, urinalysis, lung capacity, and other health data, and automatically prints out the results. Results of other tests which are not automated are also recorded in the computer.
>
> If any of the findings are abnormal, the computer signals a warning, and the patient is referred to his personal physician for further examination. In this way, preventive health monitoring can be performed by medical technicians, without involving a doctor until diagnosis is required.

The first such installation was set up as part of the War on Poverty in 1966 at the Columbia Point Health Center of Tufts University in Boston. From the moment the first patient entered the door, the computer was made to work. All pertinent information on each of the more than 6,000 residents of the community being served by the center was already in the computer's memory. The computer had assigned each resident a unique number, and a plastic card to serve as his or her Health Center ID.

The card accompanied the patient through the center on every visit, and was used, much as a credit card is, to record special slips noting his or her contacts with nurses, doctors and other staff members, the amount of time spent with each, and what lab tests, diagnoses and drug orders his treatment had entailed, all of this subsequently fed to the computer. At the end of a week, a month or any other interval, the computer could tell the Health Center staff which patients and families had used the services and which had not, and to note the differences, demographically, between the users and nonusers. It listed all the illnesses in the population, and reported how much care each member required for treatment. The system instantly identified all those who had diabetes, heart disease or any other ailment, or checked off all the households in which any one illness occurred. Neither patients nor staff were to be affected by the computer in the way the work went on day by day.

By checking on diagnoses, the tests ordered and the prescriptions written by each physician, the computer conducted a "medical audit" to secure the best possible performance by each of the doctors. The computer ran an inventory control of the pharmacy and laboratory and automatically billed welfare and other supporting agencies for the services of the center.

From the start, Drs. Count D. Gibson, Jr., and H. Jack Geiger, project directors, had high hopes for the program.

> The computer data will be important [one said], because for the first time we will have a running record of illnesses, the health needs and the medical care usage of a total population whose characteristics are known. It also will give us accurate information on the real costs of comprehensive health care. It should help us identify and correct any deficiencies of our own and help measure our progress from year to year.

These tasks were important from the start, since the Health Center was a research and demonstration project which was to serve as a prototype for other low-income urban areas.

And three important developments arose from the system: two very beneficial—multiphasic screening and the working model of a health maintenance organization—and a third, indifferently good and bad in that the system institutionalized a personally identifiable central file—to many the curtain-raiser to *1984*.

According to Bruce E. Stangle in the MIT study of security:

> The information processing capabilities of the computer allow health organizations to consider large-scale applications which could . . . revolutionize patient care, but which also present serious problems in the area of individual privacy. It is not outside the realm of possibility that in the future all patient records from every hospital, clinic, or other health organization could be shared. The advantages of such a database are clear when a doctor must treat a new patient or especially in an emergency when the doctor is not familiar with the patient's history and the patient is not able

to give this information. Equally as clear, though, is the potential threat to personal privacy present in such a database. Without proper protection, the database could be read by anyone with access to the computer. . . . Consider the impact of appointment information leaks. Suppose a business firm sends their employees to a clinic and one of the patients notices on the CRT screen that his boss is scheduled to see a psychiatrist.

There is the vulnerability to fraud: a demographic file of patients in a treatment center could represent a saleable commodity that a programmer, hard-pressed or dishonest or both, could turn over to a direct-mail firm for a neat return on no investment. And detection could be impossible, since nothing but copies from storage need be removed. And there's the touchy, life-and-death question of accuracy, to quote Stangle again:

Assume a patient were allergic to penicillin but for some reason (data input error, accidental modification, or deliberate tampering) the patient's automated record reports no such allergy. The patient goes into shock and dies after a penicillin inoculation administered by a doctor who thought the medical record was correct.

Stangle concludes that many of these "threats would pertain to noncomputer systems as well. The difference is that with computerized systems one may be able to bring data security under tighter control and thus successfully deter these threats."

Well, EDP is Mr. Stangle's business and security his bag. Still, electronic or not, secure and programmatically error-free or not, data other than what a doctor observes and knows firsthand have to be subject to doubt. Even that sometimes is. It might be argued that failure to base judgments on electronic data and readings from solid-state instruments may be as faulty as putting total faith in them. That last leap of reason, with machines or not, would seem forever to have to be subjective—the best case for action on understood grounds.

Meanwhile, fairly bold, some might think extravagantly so, research goes on in medicine with electronics. The work of José M. R. Delgado with radio-controlled brain implants is well known. Neurophysiology, indeed, has seemed to grow as a science with the growth and development of electronics and the computer. According to Leonard A. Stevens in *Explorers of the Brain*:

From Galvani's time on, knowledge of the nervous system has increased at speeds determined largely by the rate of technological innovations. It was comparatively slow in the last century and the first decades of this century; however, the early accomplishments were stupendous when one considers the limitations imposed upon neurological scientists by primitive tools such as the early galvanometers. In recent decades, especially with the coming of electronics, the rate of innovation has increased rapidly, and with their amazing new tools, neuroscientists have moved to the most important and formidable of all scientific frontiers, that which still lies between body and mind.

The work of the UCLA Brain Research Institute under the direction of Dr. John D. French illustrates the " 'interdepartmental attack upon problems' . . . wherein neurophysiologists were benefiting from applied mathematics, communication engineering, and computer analysis."

According to Dr. French, the institute's work

recognizes the current developments in these fields which render obsolete older methods of treating such data as EEG tracings or oscilloscopic recordings. Mathematicians, engineers and computer specialists join with neurophysiologists in attacking these problems collaboratively by employing skills of the physical and biological sciences which, in the recent past, would hardly have been considered complementary.

The home terminal: reluctant breakthrough

In the early stages of a technology, so many false starts may be made, so many promises can turn out illusions. The home terminal, two-way interaction between central computer and an adapted television set, may be one of the most elusive, most bewildering of the concepts to have grown up around the computer. In 1975, the idea showed every sign of simply not "taking," at least according to the rosy plans for it at the start of this decade. Strong electronics companies have in this time backed up experiments with home terminals in one form or another in Orlando, Florida; El Segundo, California, and elsewhere. Hardware costs have gone down: chips that would have cost five or six hundred dollars in 1972 cost fifty or sixty in 1975. But home terminals didn't go on the air coast to coast or even go "big" in any major city.

The recession and tight money intervened. And hardware economies for once weren't the answer. Perhaps terminals won't get into the home at all, except accidentally or after they've made their way elsewhere—in schools, libraries, government and industry or by some other than the expected means. Ma Bell's not asleep. Till a full-blown information system, like the *Times* Information Bank, plus a shopping service that takes in *all* the major consumer outlets in a region, plus income tax and home-budgeting programs and software, is made accessible to the residential subscriber at something like $10 a month, can the prospect of home terminals be seriously entertained. Typical costs for the first year of service, including terminal installation and normal use to the subscriber of the *New York Times* system, are $12,000 in New York and $18,000 on the West Coast. It's said that the *Times* Information Bank is paying its way; it has doubled the number of journals it abstracts in less than two years. It has important clients, mostly large corporations and institutions.

There's reason for bearishness and reason too to turn away from the usual nonsense about "electronic polling" and elections, anticipatory democracy, and letting your fingers do the walking through TouchTone dialing. Computer buffs and future freaks are fond of treating the public to scenes in somebody's average home that go like this:

You pick up your phone, touch a few buttons and place your handset in a special coupler in the teletypewriter terminal. Within seconds, you're on the line to "your own" computer. A few minutes later your tax returns have been calculated, the form has been printed and automatically forwarded to the IRS with a hard copy in front of you to keep for your record. Later in the day your wife (it's the hubby's machine; women can't own them, apparently) follows the same inquiry procedure through the telephone and receives a printout of some specialized recipes from among several data banks she subscribes to. She also requests information from Consumers Union on their latest evaluation of the potency of several types of vitamins. Later in the evening one of your children uses the computer terminal to receive information on a special oceanography report he is completing from the *Encyclopaedia Britannica* data bank. Your other child spends several minutes at the terminal completing her assignments in mathematics and statistics. Later you again press a few of the TouchTone buttons to inquire about and receive the latest "newspaper" information on the political scene, the standings in pro football and the forecasts for the coming weekend games, and an in-depth report on the latest evaluation of two companies you're thinking of investing in. When you've evaluated the evaluation, you enter an order for 200 shares of Ocean Protein, Inc.—a real comer. The amount of the purchase—$25.00 at 12½ cents a share plus brokerage commission—is automatically forwarded to your broker and deducted from your account without the need to send a check or to leave your comfortable, relaxovibrator chair.

Meanwhile, in the real world, time-sharing—upon which an eventual home-terminal system will have to rely—grows even more rapidly than the machines themselves. Control Data Corporation is a case in point. Benefiting from a court order in 1973, CDC bought the Service Bureau Corporation from IBM. According to CDC's 1974 annual report, service business had risen from a little over $100 million in 1970 to more than $300 million in 1973. In 1974, the first full year after the sale, CDC's billings for services were close to $400 million. International Data Corporation, a clearinghouse for industry information and publisher of the respected trade weekly *Computerworld*, estimates revenues for computer services industry-wide to have been $2.2 billion in 1973. Shaving their projections to account for the recession, the amount billed for computer services in 1975 probably was close to $3.2 billion. Control Data's service network, Cybernet, combines twenty large multiprocessing systems with thirty batch terminals, and interconnects these with customer terminals numbering in the thousands. Communications are by way of local telephones and dedicated lines (open only to Cybernet calls). The system operates in North America, Europe, Australia, and Brazil.

The remote terminals are, of course, interactive (both input and output), and they afford either graphic displays or alphanumerics, or both, as well as keyboards and nonimpact printers. With time-sharing the user is in control of all parts of the system that are needed to carry out the work he is doing. Though he has only the CRT, the keyboard and the printer, it's as if he had the use of the mainframe all to himself. It is, for this reason, called a virtual machine, a simulation of an operating system that is exclusively the user's—inoperable for others, though others, thousands of others, can be accessing the mainframe at the same time he is, and all of them operating their own virtual machines. Time-sharing is an extension of multiprogramming—a computer working on several programs at one time, which in itself is an extension of parallel operation as opposed to serial. There is a real distinction between the concepts. Multiprogramming refers to parallel processing within one integral system, and time-sharing, to making available the multiprogramming facilities of the control unit to more than one system or to a network of users.

Engineers can enter design specifications into the terminal, and the computer projects these on the CRT. The engineer can correct the display with his light pen (or stylus). A "window into the computer," the pen generates a pulse. When touched or put close to the screen, the pen's movements are interpreted as corrections to the display and, hence, to the information, whether graphic or alphanumeric, that is being processed. Curves drawn are mathematically smoothed to compensate for the inevitable unsteadiness of the human hand. The operator may delete, add or change the information. Three-dimensional views may be turned to show varying angles of the design, in correct perspective each time. Once plotted on the screen, either by the pen or by mathematical coordinates entered by way of the keyboard, drawings may be stored—in original and revised versions—in memory devices associated with the terminal or with the computer. Tape cassettes containing the basic digital information can be played back when the engineer wants to modify the design or to display it for demonstrations in conferences. These are only the most obvious aspects of computer-aided design. The usefulness of correctible and turnable geometric display in teaching mathematics at any level is easy to see. It's tempting to think of computer graphics as a toy in the hands of the technologist, but it is, rather, a tool of value for the picturing of complicated objects and constructions and for modeling the environment or concepts in three dimensions.

In another setting, according to the *New York Times,* reporters of the future will carry portable terminals consisting of a keyboard and a CRT. The unit will transmit copy from any telephone back to the host computer. Editors in the office will have terminals too. They'll be able to call up stories onto their screens and make corrections to them by way of the keyboard. When he completes his work on a story, the editor will release it to the central computer.

The computer "reads" the copy and, through phototypesetting, turns it into positive prints from which standard printing plates can be made. Conversion to photo-offset printing is under consideration by the *Times* (many newspapers already use it) for the obvious advantage of being able to go from the made-up pages of film directly to the presses. Again we're racing a moving target. Nonimpact, xerographic printing may very soon be usable on large, long-run presses and so make obsolete the very latest improvements in offset printing.

"The private secretary will all but disappear," an article in *Administrative Management* announced in 1973. She'll be a craftsman no longer needed in an age of automation, her letters being put together by word-processing machines and systems. Rita Reif writes in the *Times* (May 4, 1975):

> The evolution of the typewriter from a machine operated by hands and feet [as in the first machines by Sholes and Glidden of 1873] to one that, without either, zooms along typing 350 words a minute makes automation in the office seem a flick of the switch away.

Once the mainstay of the office equipment industry and still at the center of office routine, the manual typewriter is seen to be "going the way of buggy whips and fountain pens." Reif's report goes on:

> The manual . . . is, of course, incapable of linking up with [or keeping up with] the electric machines that dominate modern word-processing developments. . . . Today [these include] typewriters linked to card or cassette tape recorders and typewriters hooked up to other typewriters via telephone. Other processors utilize the typewriter as a computer terminal or as text-editing machines [like those Ms. Reif's company proposes to install]. . . . The most complex and costly word processors, selling for up to $100,000, are those that relay to, and accept data from,

computers or that tie into printing equipment. The one function that has not been automated is the initial typing task.

The first step along the road to typing automation occurred within the machine: the changeover from type bars and a moving carriage to the moving type ball as perfected in the famous Selectric, introduced by IBM in 1961. According to Reif:

> But what the type ball offered in stepped-up machine speed was only a partial answer to mushrooming office needs. . . . Typing studies have shown that erasures, corrections and retyping can slow the average . . . speed to 10 or 11 words a minute. Automation of paper processed began in 1964 when I.B.M. hitched the Selectric to a magnetic tape recorder, an updated application of the player-piano roll (magnetic cards followed in 1969) on which the typist's function is reduced to doing the initial typing and corrections. Both are fed into the recorder and the corrected document is automatically retyped at 150 words a minute. Today such assisted typewriters cost up to $6,000.

Since 1972, when "word processing" caught on as a selling catch-phrase, a score of companies in the office-equipment and electronics field have introduced a number of innovations ostensibly improving on the Selectric and extending the basic concept. There is now a whirling, radially spiked disk called the "daisy." Xerox's model 800 incorporates the daisy, and so do a number of other machines introduced in 1974 and 1975. They double the speed of the ball. And really when it comes to machines with daisies, the word *typewriter* goes into disuse. With speeds of 350 words a minute, and even of 540, we're dealing with what the industry calls a printer. Typical of these is one called the Qume.

These are all impact machines. Higher-speed nonimpact versions and (when they're perfected) impact machines that work in parallel rather than bit-by-bit or character-by-character in raster fashion (as in TV scanning) are more compatible with terminal and computer speeds. Nonimpact printers on the market or under development include ink jet and xerography using regular paper, and thermal, electrostatic and electrochemical on treated paper. Speeds on nonimpact printers have reached as high as 45,000 characters per second (on the IBM 3800 electrophotographic subsystem). That comes to 10,000 pages an hour, each page 8½" x 11" fan-folded (of the computer-printout type). The book business just might hear about this and see in it a workable means of achieving "publishing on demand."

Government Executive for January 1974 takes a hard look at the whole subject. This journal for government office managers points out that paperwork takes a big bite from corporate profits and from government budgets as well. The cost of doing a business letter has risen from two dollars in the early sixties to anywhere from four to sixteen dollars at the time of writing. And the situation, the publication just about groans, is no better in government, as well it would be expected not to be.

IBM's definition of word processing and a terse explanation are offered:

". . . a combination of people, procedures and equipment that transforms ideas into printed communications and facilitates the flow of related office work . . . at a savings over prior methods, when properly organized and managed." . . . An administrator who wants to dictate a letter picks up a regular telephone instrument, dials a designated number of digits, and dictates his letter. The letter is recorded on a magnetic belt in a PBX [private branch exchange] Recorder located in a special room called a Word Processing Center. A word processing secretary removes the magnetic belt, places it on a transcriber, and transcribes the letter in draft form. Using a magnetic media typewriter rather than an ordinary electric typewriter, transcription speed rises to about 30 words per minute. As the letter is typed, it is recorded on a magnetic tape or . . . card. This allows the typist to work at rough draft speed, correcting errors by merely backspacing and retyping over the error.

. . . After the draft letter has been typed and corrections made, proper stationery is positioned by the secretary and the letter is "played out" on an automatic typewriter at a rate of 150 words per minute in the number of copies required.

The journal concludes that:

> . . . The impact of word processing in this decade might best be equated to the impact that was [made] by electronic data processing in the Sixties.

Computer-aided instruction

No matter the plight of the secretary or clerk typist, the teacher's not going any day soon into the dustbin of the technologically displaced, but he or she certainly is mindful of the seismic impact of electronics on the young. From the textbooks and courses built on the principles of programmed, fortified or structured learning and teaching machines to computer-aided instruction (CAI), interactive techniques have had much to do with recent teaching methods. At every level in school, students have been seen to benefit from periodic sessions with terminals. The machines are programmed to talk with the student by CRT or printer. There's nothing cute about the machine's manner; mostly it's a brass-tacks pacing of the program to the individual's strengthening grasp of a subject.

On the college level, one of the earliest, and most ambitious for its time, computer networks of any kind, according to Robert F. Hargraves, was and is the Dartmouth Time-Sharing System (DTSS). Indeed, DTSS was the forerunner of General Electric's global system, the world's largest. When DTSS was first put to work in 1964, it was decided

> . . . that exposure to computing and free availability of computing should become a standard part of the liberal arts education at Dartmouth, and in the undergraduate college where

> only 25 per cent of the students elect majors in the sciences and engineering. . . . Against this background, it was recognized that the user-computer interface had to be simplified and harmonized with the educational environment if liberal arts students were to ingest a reasonable dose of sensible knowledge about computing. Two important consequences . . . were the decisions to bring the computer to the student via remote individual terminals . . . and to devise an extremely simple user interface.

Also on the college level, there are more recent time-sharing systems like those installed by Honeywell at the University of Waterloo (Ontario) and at the U.S. Military Academy at West Point. Ostensibly, any subject reducible in one phase of the course or another to a step-by-step progression through a series of questions is suitable for CAI programming. Beyond are more sophisticated uses of the technique in advanced studies, especially in mathematics and in the statistical aspects of the sciences.

Teachers in math classes at West Point, for instance, access the computer from terminals and produce drawings on the classroom screen or in hard copies, printed-paper duplicates, to illustrate and augment explanations. Using the terminal, the teacher might enter a function in integral calculus, the limits and the values, and the computer would generate the drawing derived from the function on the classroom screen. As part of the demonstration, the teacher may change the values or enter new ones, and another drawing will appear to show the graphic response to the change in variables.

The academy, unknown to many perhaps, has a fine collection of first editions of William Faulkner and other memorabilia relating to the great novelist. The computer there is running materials for a Faulkner concordance. As a matter of fact, the world of the humanities is no stranger to the world of electronic quantification. Among the instances, too many to list, is the making of dictionaries—a subject nicely introduced in a short piece written by Henry Kučera of Brown University that appears in *The American Heritage Dictionary of the English Language*, and another that gives a more detailed report of a later, more extensive use of computerized lexicography, in the introduction to *The American Heritage School Dictionary*. These attempts, admittedly, are beginnings only, not yet scratching a CRT, so to speak, for they're batch processing. What will open to linguistic studies when theories such as those of Noam Chomsky are put onto realtime interaction is anyone's guess. Programs for forming concordances of a writer's works and for generating word lists and examples of usage, as was done twice so effectively by American Heritage staffs, are fairly simple. And this in no way belittles their importance. Still, devising a system that will parse a sentence—tell how it's structured, how each word in it behaves—has yet to be done to any satisfactory extent. This lack affects computerized translation. Word equivalents between languages can be handled, but there's no way yet to transform by computer the deep (underlying, regardless of form) meaning of an English sentence into the surface forms of another language. The transformation from deep to surface structure is, indeed, yet to be achieved on a machine within one language, let alone from one to another.

Again, as for computers on the campus, along with the banks, the airlines and the military, universities have played a pivotal part in the development of computer-and-terminal networks—a subliminal constellation of forces that was not lost on campus demonstrators of recent memory.

chapter 00100

The Robots Are Coming —and Giants Too

Networks of computers, large and small, don't bring together arrays of terminals alone. They also coordinate work forces of sensing and performing tools and machines—the automatons, robots, smart machines and intelligent factories. And these sensing, behaving and self-correcting units are among them, closing in on the divide between man and his implements.

With their swinging arms and twisting hands, the robots are programmed to do any number of mechanical jobs, and to do them the same way over and over to within 1/10,000th of an inch of specifications. The arms, fists and fingers are as rugged as they are tireless, doing work as sanders, punches and drills. And their TV-camera eyes recognize and react to colors, shapes and patterns. Some robots, when they're running low on power, search for, locate and plug themselves into wall outlets for a recharging. Starting with a raw sheet of metal, a certain robot, Lulu (not its real name), shapes and finishes automobile fenders—replacing twenty men on the job.

To train, or program, a robot, you put it through its paces under manual control. The machine's memory drum stores all the discrete details of position, movement and attitude, and then puts the robot to work, automatically, through all the repeated steps and cycles. The programming takes just minutes ordinarily; the machine goes on doing the routine, without forgetting or altering a wink till it's ordered to stop or shut off.

Interesting theories, from a number of scientific disciplines, back up the workings of robots. Stemming from his study of recursion in numbers—each new step or difference in a series being derived from the results of previous differences—Alan Turing, working with Emil Post, postulated a universal automaton, one of the proverbial "black boxes," which operates on an infinite web of tape that contains an infinite series of binary states. A "universal turing machine," as the notion has come to be called, exists, as Goldstine explains,

> . . . in the sense that it can calculate any sequence that any special automaton can, provided only that it receives the appropriate set of input orders. This seems paradoxical, since in principle one can imagine automata of varying sizes and complexities. However, [Turing] showed it is true . . . that any particular automaton can be described by a finite set of instructions, and that when this is fed to his universal automaton, it in turn imitates the special one.

Turing's "proof" fired the intellect and imagination of John von Neumann, who, in the decade before his death in 1957, became something of a high-powered message center (or CPU) for the advanced mathematical and scientific ideas of the immediate postwar years. He wanted first "to find out how complex a device or construct needed to be in order to be self-reproductive, and . . . to investigate the problem of how to organize devices that must be made from parts that can malfunction." He was for a time during this period, through a group he had brought together called the Teleological Society, in touch with Warren S. McCulloch and Walter H. Pitts. They were neurophysiologists. Their paper, "A Logical Calculus of the Ideas Immanent in Nervous Activity," furnished exciting leads to the early computer architect: "anything that can be exhaustively and unambiguously described, anything that can be completely and unambiguously put into words, is ipso facto realizable by a suitable finite neural network . . ." In 1948 came Claude Shannon's "A Mathematical Theory of Communication"—information theory, an adaptation of the laws of thermodynamics to the behavior of messages in transmission. It was ". . . something of a delayed action bomb," as John R. Pierce has put it, and according to Brockway McMillan:

> Shannon's model describes, in universally applicable terms that are independent of the physical details of any particular transmission system, the two essential elements of the communications process. First is the message source, representing the collection, or statistical universe, of all possible messages that conceivably could be offered for transmission; with each is associated its own probability of occurrence.
>
> Second is the transmission channel, which at its input accepts signals and at its output presents approximate versions of those signals—perturbed, however, by noise introduced in the transmission. The manner in which the noise perturbs the signal is also presented in completely general terms as something governed only by statistical laws. . . .
>
> And from Shannon's theory came the fundamental result that no one had foreseen: that even a noisy channel, having limited bandwidth and a limited power level, had a non-zero capacity for error-free transmission.

Von Neumann grasped the relevance to computers. His specific interests were in the Air Force's problem of missile reliability and in how the human nervous system allows us to work reliably even though individual neurons may be unreliable. He grasped the connections, but, as Goldstine points out, he was inherently dissatisfied with his own procedure, and in 1952 he said during a lecture at California Institute of Technology:

> . . . error should be treated by thermodynamical methods, and be the subject of a thermodynamical theory, as information has been, by the work of L. Szilard and C. E. Shannon. . . . The present treatment falls far short of achieving this, but it assembles, it is hoped, some of the building materials which will have to enter into the final structure.

In effect, it did all come together, at about the time of von Neumann's death and within several years thereafter. There were papers by Peter Elias, and by S. Winograd and J. D. Cowan, which, in Goldstine's words again,

> surely would have been viewed by von Neumann as carrying out his program to the end. . . . [What] they did was to adapt Shannon's ideas on information to computation. To do this they succeeded in defining the notion of computational capacity for unreliable modules . . . and showed that arbitrarily reliable networks may be built out of such modules using a module redundancy that "need only be greater [quoting Winograd and Cowan] than a certain minimum whose value is determined by the computation capacity of modules comprising these networks."

In 1959, "What the Frog's Eye Tells the Frog's Brain" was published, with McCulloch and Pitts among the author-researchers. What von Neumann might have known of the work that backed up the study, we don't know. However, the conclusions, as drawn by Leonard A. Stevens in *Explorers of the Brain,* point up the analogy to automatons and computing:

> What the frog sees is not a function of the brain alone, but of the nerve cells between the eye and brain. In brief, the ganglion cells with their fibers forming the optic nerve are more than simple transmitters of information. They also seem to be able to think about and act on the messages that are en route to the brain.

—much like the salivary glands of Pavlov's dog (pages 29–30).

And not too unlike the computer hand developed at Stanford University. It has the ability to observe and manipulate its environment and, under programming, to accept a number of spoken commands. Its eye is an ordinary TV camera coupled to a monitor. The hand is able, under direction, to trace the contours of an object such as a cube, to grip it, move it about and place it intelligently—that is, reasonably, where it's supposed to. The process is a primitive, idiotically simple, or complex (however you look at it) synthesis of the steps a man takes in performing the same maneuver: sight object, touch, grasp, lift, move, find similar objects in new location, place, go back for more. The disturbing thing about it is the silent, relentless, energy-saving efficiency.

Unimate is perhaps the best known of the commercial robots in America. It's a one-armed, hydraulic and pneumatic mechanism controlled by an electromagnetic memory drum. The machines are the brainchild of George C. Devol, who took out his first patents for them in the 1950s. He saw that the pushbutton society had to be taken one step further. The number of start-and-stop, put-and-take operations in factories suggested to him that the rationalization of these processes could hypothetically be put on one of Turing's tapes and the tape left to instruct machines to do the jobs heretofore imposed on man. By 1974, through actual trial, development and production for over a decade, the series 2000 Unimate had become the stakhanovite of the line.

The Unimate can store up to 180 separate commands. Each command may encompass a sequence of five spatial variants. The arm, under hydraulic power, has an effective reach of from $3\frac{1}{2}$ to $7\frac{1}{2}$ feet, and it can lift and carry objects weighing as much as 75 pounds through an arc of 220 degrees. Burdens of 25 pounds and less can be carried at the machine's top speed. A heavy-duty alternate, the series

4000, does all that the 2000 does, and handles up to 350 pounds. The jointed hand at the end of the arm can swivel independently an additional 180 degrees, giving it the power to turn objects upside down. There is a theoretical infinity of positions possible within the five axes of motion—up-down, in-out, rotation, wrist-twist and wrist-bend. Objects can be placed within a margin of error of less than a sixteenth of an inch (0.05″ actually is the specification).

The manual work-through of the motions is all the programming that's required. Depending on instructions, the machine can automatically recycle itself to repeat a procedure or shut itself off and be ready to start again on signal. It can be made to control other equipment or to respond to commands from other machines. It's eminently responsive and articulate, one might say; an obedient servant and faithful companion. Changes may be made in part of the program of instructions without having to completely retrain the Unimate. And programs can be held on cassettes and stored. This way, even the brief training time—usually about twenty minutes—need not be repeated when new work has to be processed the same way at a later time. Indeed, Unimate is unique among production-line machines in that it doesn't have to be retooled or scrapped to take care of model changes. The machine remains the same; the instructions change; and, on cassettes, these instructions can be used on any Unimate, not just on the one that recorded them. One machine can be made to train another, in fact, and theoretically be a better teacher than a technician, since what it teaches is exactly what it has been taught.

There is an extensive "library" of hands available, each with distinctive sets of articulation, especially suited to particular tasks. Generally, Unimate is the logical choice for operations of the transfer type that are too heavy or dangerous and exacting for humans, and too "sophisticated" for other automatic machines. Extreme heat, moisture, noise, fumes, even isolation don't affect performance.

Unimation, Inc., publishes the comments of users, and they offer a pretty good idea of the range of applications and of the reasons people give for putting robots to work:

> Payout time with our first Unimate was less than nine months . . . If the robot is going to pay off for us, it has to run two machines. And it does. . . . We have much less repair work on molds, because with the robot we have an automated lubricator. . . . The robot takes the place of the die-casting operator and the trim-press operator. . . . About this new occupational safety act: if we have a robot operating the die-casting machine, we don't have a safety problem. Now if you don't have to protect a man, you have a savings of about $20,000 worth of safety equipment that you don't have to put on the machine. And the way we use a robot for unloading two die-casting machines, you can figure a robot pays for itself as soon as you buy it. . . . One of the strong points is the total repeatability from cycle to cycle. . . . No problem with men. We have one man who takes care of seven Unimates plus five other machines and nobody says we shouldn't have them. Nobody worries about their jobs. Matter of fact, we keep hiring. But now, instead of putting on two people, we hire one and put a Unimate on. Set-up time? No sweat. It takes us two, maybe two and a half minutes [!] to put a new die on and teach the Unimate. . . .

By mid-1974 Unimate robots had accumulated more than half a million hours of operating experience. Unimates have been used to apply porcelain enameling and paint by spray during the making of appliances, automobiles and lighting fixtures; their smooth, continuous motion is especially good at putting a coating on intricately shaped parts. They were being used to load a variety of machine tools; they were operating heat-treating equipment without supervision in an atmosphere of fumes where no human could work; they were on line at refractories and kilns, making precision die-castings. And Unimates have a delicate touch: a team of them were being used to pack glass tubing in harsh furnace surroundings. After the uprising at Lordstown, Ohio, in the General Motors assembly plant, both the Unimates and the rebellious workers had by 1975 settled into a (arm's length? unarticulated?) truce.

Needless to say, Unimates aren't the only tribe in the robotic race. At a new Volvo plant in Sweden, robots outnumber human workers by 400 to 60, and they do all the hard work. With uncanny precision, the waist-high red robots there in turn pick up an engine block, move silently off to the first section of the assembly area and stop obediently by the side of a worker. He or she (half the force are women) makes some adjustments or adds a part and releases the robot with a turn of the starter handle. The robot moves on to the next section and, section by section, on to the end.

When assembly is completed the robot glides off with the finished engine into the testing shop. There it unfailingly selects the first vacant test position and stops. Afterward, the cycle complete, it makes its way back through the maze of machines to the starting point and joins the line of robots waiting silently for their turn to pick up another engine block.

As eerily efficient as the robots look, the bosses at Volvo say there's no danger of their taking over the factory. The secret of their precise movements is the electronic brain in each and a system of magnetic tracks built into the floor. They do the bidding of the workers, who, like those at the Saab plant in Södertälje, decide among themselves what work norms to set for the plant. The whole Volvo plant, including the robots at a cost of $2,000 apiece, was planned jointly by management and the workers. A Volvo official has said: "One of the problems for management today is that the old discipline doesn't work and we have very few things to replace it with. But we are dealing with educated people who are perfectly capable as individuals of taking initiative."

Under experimentation at the California Institute of Technology: a robot optical system, complete with laser eye, photocell "retina," copper "optic nerve" and electronic brain. It is capable of doing a host of coarse sorting jobs: fingerprints, handwriting and voice waveforms on oscilloscopes. In biomedical tests, the system readily distinguishes dystrophic from healthy muscle tissue.

The foreman in the usual factory walks his feet off down on the factory floor and still has but a rough idea of the productivity of his workers and machines. Daily reports are a hassle and subject to error and wishful thinking. An operator may struggle with a balky machine for hours before admitting defeat, never realizing the cost to the company of all the lost production. Yet most production machines, especially those in metal-working, plastic-forming, printing and packaging, involve simple repetitive motions that can readily be monitored and tallied. Counters, mounted directly on the machine or actuated by the operator, represent one of the oldest and most reliable data-acquisition techniques used by industry. From them have grown, in recent years, various schemes for centralizing the data and converting it into a format that would be of immediate use to production supervisors. One of the most ambitious of these is AMS-3, a machine-monitoring system developed by Space Craft of Greenville, South Carolina.

AMS-3 incorporates a minicomputer which generates a running account of production in a plant. On command it can provide up-to-the-minute reports on the number of machines working, those that are down, for how long and why, the number of pieces produced by each and by lot number, the cost per part as a function of wages and machine time. At the end of a shift the computer prints out a report. The same data serve as a source for automatically adjusting inventory, calculating payrolls, scheduling maintenance, and performing other administrative functions.

The minicomputer is not intrusive. All the foremen have to do is enter shift numbers, machine assignments and other data on a simple control panel. The software is built in and needs no in-plant supervision.

Most of the reporting is on a routine basis, but the foreman can enter requests for information on given machines or operators by simply pressing the right buttons. There are alarms to signal slowdowns or downtime or when a machine is being operated without authorization.

Sensors and transducers at each machine take analog readings—of flow rates, pressures and waveforms—and digitize them for processing. To cut down on the wiring throughout the factory, messages to and from the machine stations are multiplexed—coded and transmitted at the same time through the same channels. Terminals at each station contain simplified keyboards and slots for worker ID cards. The worker uses these to enter his own number and that of the production lot he's working on.

AMS-3 is process control; it provides the means for controlling a whole system of production. Numerical control (NC) computers, on the other hand, work on the level of the individual machine or work station. An NC machine might select a dozen tools in succession in a typical fifteen-minute sequence in order to smooth off the edges of a piece of steel, cut grooves through its center and bore a hole through the top—all steps in the making, say, of the parts for printing presses. NC computers run lathes, milling machines and punch presses at accuracies to the minutest tolerances and at speeds and efficiencies never thought possible. Numerical control allows a machine, like a lathe, to run by itself, unattended, following a binary-coded program that instructs it on positioning the workpiece, setting chucks and jaws, selecting tools—without a man's having to set up, change adjustments, stop the work when it's finished or place new pieces for continuing the process. Any changes in work flow relate only to machines and programs, and not to the vagaries of temperament, health and the weather.

Electronics firms are especially attracted to numerical control because of major cost reductions, consistently higher quality and the ease it affords in making engineering changes during new product development. Indeed, numerical control turns any machine into a robot: it makes parts, it makes tools; in broader applications, it assembles. Furthermore, it's not tied to mass production but can work on a short-order, one-at-a-time footing.

Executives everywhere have been quick to see that the right mix of microprocessors and minicomputers, running individual machines and whole factories, at low cost and with little or no programming, makes the big difference between profit and loss. This is important especially to plants that sell any sizeable portion of their output abroad where they have to compete with low-cost, Third World labor. Numerical control and other computer-aided production is important in the Third World too where there's a shortage of skilled workers. Automation can conceivably allow a poor country to leap over any gaps in technology and to arrive full-blown in the computer age, ripe with a cadre of trained programmers who need undergo nothing like the Westerner's apprenticeships in machine and materials handling. Be that as it may, it's a surprise in plants large and small in North America, Europe and Japan *not* to see islands of automation running all or good parts of the show.

Like the aircraft carrier, which is 5 percent control island and 95 percent flight deck, the model of the modern factory is functional in the extreme. Through networks of control mechanisms, it withdraws the human hand and eye from the work space and leaves the takeoffs and landings of goods and products to run out on their own the endless, alterable tape of programmed consumption.

Apart from obvious boosts to productivity through making the individual worker more efficient and apart from keeping a ceiling on the work force, automated operations provide other savings. They tend to produce less scrap and pollution and fewer rejects, and to require less reworking, less in-process inventory, less clerical and administrative backup, and less space than the conventional methods of work. And these often considerable savings are not confined to manufacturing industries. One bank found that centralized data processing permitted smaller new branch offices and cut building costs by 15 percent, far more than estimated at the time of the decision to install EDP.

Automatic production equipment in former years was efficient enough to pay for itself in less than five years. Today, we find many instances of reductions in payout down to two years—for many robots, to less than one. Many companies say too, or imply, that they automate, "go computer," to improve the quality of their output, their customer service, or their image—all important factors in competition, as full-page ads attest. Computers in banks, car rental agencies, airlines, auto repair shops are pluggable, to be flaunted.

The decision might address particular problems: unmanageable and increasing volumes of paperwork and clerical turnover in banks, for one example; temporary labor in warehouses, for another. Automation can mitigate losses from pilferage and breakage—marginal factors maybe, but not insignificant. Wall Street brokerages aren't the only firms to have barely survived a paper crunch. The backup of red tape that brought the stock market to a virtual halt in the sixties is a moral tale to many. Clerical employees, from management's point of view, are here today, gone tomorrow, easily (but expensively) replaced, apathetic, prone to error and false consciousness, a Marxian's way of saying that they have their minds on themselves and not the job or the major issues. Well-designed software and adequate EDP produce the needed flow of information far more consistently and expeditiously.

As for the effect on employment, savings accrue in labor-intensive industries that opt for automation since the work forces grow less rapidly than they would ordinarily. Indirect labor costs like employee recruitment and training are reduced. The relationship is now inverse, as we've seen: production swells, the work force shrinks. Moreover, fewer temporary employees and fewer hours of overtime are needed to cope with normal fluctuations in volume.

Management attains a better grasp of its costs, a better measure of them and the means to keep them stable even as output increases; nearly all investments in automation pay for themselves—as advertised, as forecast, by the equipment suppliers, independent consultants and in-house studies. These all take their slices, and the rest is gravy. That's the megillah.

Decisions are freer and better informed. Retooling and rescheduling for changes in design and demand, especially with a combination of numerical and process control, may take place on short notice, and safely, with all the timely, reliable information at one's disposal. Marketing and promotion are greatly facilitated, and so are budget changes. As management gains confidence and sees that automation can reduce and solve operational problems, it becomes less and less likely or willing to live with them. Success with automation and stories of success with it that appear in the trade press make the move to automate an easy one. Articles and conferences devoted to the subject multiply, and the exposure favors more and more conversions, though decisions will still be based (if only as a matter of form) on detailed studies.

Another thing feeding the trend is the cross-fertilization that goes on across industry lines. What works in one area can be adapted and used in another. Wherever one looks, the well-known factors are at work: (1) the rapid development of microprocessing technology; (2) the reduced costs of electronic devices generally; (3) the availability of suitable software; (4) the publicized successes of the computer in slowing the escalation of human costs and their consequent squeeze on profits; and (5) tax breaks for purchases of capital equipment.

Labor turnover is no small expense. There are (1) the time lost and the drop in efficiency during the period between one employee's separation and his replacement; (2) the interviews, tests and selection of the replacement; (3) the initial training; (4) the differential between a new person's salary and his slowness in rising to proper productivity; (5) the reduced productivity of other workers while the replacement works himself into the scheme of things; (6) the lost productivity of capital equipment that remains intermittently idle in the absence of full manning; (7) moving the new person into a new house if that becomes part of the deal. On the last point alone, an Atlas Van Lines survey in 1972 showed that a company spends an average of $2,459 to move an employee. More than that, nearly three of five corporations offered a transferred employee assistance in disposing of his old house, either by guaranteeing its sale, by paying broker's and lawyer's fees or by buying it outright.

With human costs reduced or out of the question, increased automation can mean more efficient production and better goods to the consumer at lower prices. This engenders competition, and there's added drive to solve operational problems and to increase flexibility. In a good, well-ordered world, society might benefit from it all. This is funny, though it's not supposed to be. Eric Berne cites somewhere the survey of hospital staff attitudes, the conclusion of which was that everything would work so much better in health care without the patients.

The electronic zap of the salesman

As networks expand, as microprocessing increases the productivity of communications lines and of computer components, even "unautomatable" occupations like sales and purchasing look less than safe. Thanks to electronic storage and transmission, almost any type of document, plan or drawing normally contained in manual filing systems can now be made available by the manufacturer to customers and prospects at their desks, homes, yachts, capsules in space, where not. The immediate dissemination of product information should suggest that a salesman's traveling and the number of calls he makes can be reduced. It might also suggest that, in effect, fewer salesmen will be needed.

The "sourcing" that a purchasing agent does entails a continuing study of the materials and services his company has to buy. The information required can come to the purchasing department as requested from the vendor's database, with little or no human intervention if automatic systems are in force. Purchasing departments are often part of an inventory control program. Linked through a management information system to the firm's database, inventory control offers reports on command as to goods in stock, allocated, on order, the reorder point for each item, the economic ordering quantity and a number of other factors. A sourcing program would include a system for evaluating suppliers by a grading index. A supplier with the lowest price, for example, might receive the highest grade, ten, for that single criterion. Other criteria might be: freight rate, the reliability of the product, its quality, the vendor's terms and policies on returns, allowances and discounts. Accordingly, the system may even be programmed to issue purchase orders without direct input from a purchasing agent, unless of course an extra ten is slipped in because a supplier is related to the boss or is himself a good customer of the purchasing company. (Even such unquantifiables can be jiggered into the program.)

Indeed, on the retail level, this, aside from speeding the transaction with the customer, is what point-of-sale terminals are all about: the retailer's main computer can place a direct order with an elected supplier's terminal, and the covering documents, including a properly dated check, are completed in seconds and sent out as confirmation—all controlled automatically by the same system. The process is fast, accurate and "hourly current," and scores of accounting, clerical and middle-management people as well as reams of paper documents are *not* involved. It's even possible, as electronic funds transfer systems go into effect, that no documents at all need change hands. The only question then would be philosophical: with so much going on and no one around to observe, would anything—all that input of material and output of goods—really *be there*—like the tree that falls in the forest without anyone hearing the crash; has it really fallen?

Time-sharing computer systems with terminals have given new life to the old quip: You too can be replaced by a computer—but not so much replaced by the computer as by the young MBA who knows better than you how to use a computer and to make it his partner.

The print culture, gone electronic

McLuhan didn't do the book in, much as publishers and print freaks acted in dread as though he were going to, and electronic technology has not yet done the book in, nor foreseeably will it. The computer and the book, however, can be seen coming together. Information, especially technical, but of many sorts, in print form is now stored for instant retrieval in several libraries, and libraries have been interconnected to provide indexing to combined files. Video and microfilm display of books, reports, newspapers and periodicals, by page and paragraph on demand, are available from some limited systems.

Information retrieval works on key words and an abstract, which in a hundred words or so gives the gist of the reference. As Gordon B. Davis explains it in *Introduction to Electronic Computers* (1971):

> . . . an article about the effect of radiation on metals in the Van Allen belt might be identified by metals, radiation, Van Allen belt, and space. In addition to [these] key-word identifiers, a short abstract is prepared and stored on secondary storage medium. [A person] wishing information on a topic chooses a set of identifiers which best describe the topic. The computer is programmed to compare this set of identifiers with the list of all identifiers and to select papers having sets of identifiers containing one or more . . . common to [those of] the topic. . . . The abstracts for these papers are then printed out . . .

or displayed on the terminal, "together with an identifying number through which the article may be located." As we have seen, the *New York Times* Information Bank is typical of such a system. The next evolutionary step will be display and facsimile printouts of lengthier materials. When the densities of storage media such as holography are considered, the possibilities are staggering. Ten trillion bits of information can be recorded on a surface of holographic film measuring four feet by four feet. Theoretically, 500 million pages of a newspaper could be recorded in a second, were there a way to expose the copy at such a rate.

Computerized editing and typesetting of textbooks and all kinds of printed matter have been perfected. The computer-age newspaper, printed and delivered at the touch of a button or displayed on a CRT, is technically feasible, if not commercially ready for wide distribution. Publishers and printers of magazines have computers programmed to handle their subscription lists, their mailings and accounting, as well as to evaluate soundings of public response to their contents. The planning, scheduling and testing of advertising have been on stream for some time; computers only intensify and sophisticate the process. Outside publishing as such, many of these techniques, especially word processing, information retrieval and pattern recognition, have broad applications. Indeed, with the design, distribution and copyrighting of software packages, the computer firms and computer users become publishers in effect, and their technologies—the making of semiconductor chips, for one—turn them into lithographers, photoengravers and printers.

There are giants . . .

Computers and their satellite systems and technologies can be seen to exist for no other reason than to serve man. Yet there is more than just a hidden threat, especially in the near miracle of smart machines, terminals and industrial networks. It's tempting to conclude not only that the machines have outdistanced their creators, but also that they pose the threat of ignoring them as the crucial link in the system. Man, a frail and fickle component who deals in subjective judgments of qualities along with his rigid strings of calculations, must conceivably be mated with the boss machine or subjugated to it. This can mean confinement to cold and impersonal quantities to the exclusion of passion and judgment, or . . . ?

It's not easy to be sure. The question might make no sense and the alternative be beside the point. For what all this amounts to—the orchestration through time-sharing of the instruments of information and control, the terminals, the batches, the tapes, the lopped-corner cards that can't be missorted, the radio and telephone lines and cables—is the complete reordering of jobs and routines, everywhere. The moving target of technology also reorders the roles of the machines, the components and devices themselves, to say nothing of man's roles.

From the tiniest span in an integrated circuit one-hundredth the width of a human hair to the space-wide reach of a computer's signal, man has incorporated concepts of control that push and pull his intellect to unforeseen limits, or to limits beyond limits—in either direction, atomward and starward, to infinity. Going both ways, toward infinite densities and infinite reach, the uniting of microprocessing with any number of network configurations brings computer technology to the threshold of universal power and availability. A threshold that doesn't exist, really, but which always beckons.

Super- or maxicomputers have been with us for more than a decade—IBM's STRETCH and Univac's LARC from the late fifties. Indeed, the Defense Department's SAGE (Semiautomatic Ground Environment) was in operation in the mid-fifties, and still is. In Rein Turn's words, "It is a vast complex of radars, computers, situation displays, communication links, and man." Evaluations of threats are made by human operators on the basis of displayed tracks of what could be enemy aircraft. These are passed on to commanders and to pilots of interceptor airplanes who scramble to investigate and pursue.

Maybe we've not yet got a supernetwork. Though the networks we have are big enough—Control Data's Cybernet, IBM's Advanced Administrative System, and General Electric's Information Service—and the potentialities for building the ultimate from the base of such machines as the IBM 370/168 are with us, again we're racing a moving target, and from the evidence at hand it's impossible to conceive what the next s t r e t c h outward is to be.

As matters stand, in the quicksilver lexicography of

EDP, *supercomputer = network.* The concept is simple. A network is two or more processing units, not necessarily big machines, operating together. The microprocessors and the minicomputer in a point-of-sale installation form a network, strictly speaking. But networks as supercomputers and vice versa are really the subject here.

Control Data Corporation, the maker of one of the most advanced and most recent supers—the JPL/STAR (for Jet Propulsion Laboratory/Self-Testing and Repairing)—sees the network concept as giving birth to "the third era of information processing." First came information processing as such; second, storage and retrieval; and third, growing out of time-sharing, the movement of information. Through complex arrangements within the large systems themselves, between several large systems and between them and outlying terminals, the economies of scale gained through microprocessing reach the highest level of effectiveness.

What is primarily at work in the massive systems is redundancy, a quality that is made that much more available by the low cost of large-scale integration; so much in the way of control goes into that one tiny chip. The JPL/STAR, for instance, with a high concentration of LSI, was designed to deliver a degree of self-correcting reliability beyond the reach of conventional systems. Here's how it works: firmware in the system contains error-detecting codes; each part of the computer consists of duplicate and replaceable modules; when a module fails, power is switched from it to a ready replacement. The advantage of such a system in the managing of spaceborne computers is fairly obvious.

Another large CDC computer is the STAR 100. Essentially it is a conventional system that operates on the pipeline principle. Pipelining allows a number of operations to be performed concurrently and so increases the speed of execution, in the case of STAR 100, by a factor of eighty.
 The system, in effect, becomes a network, and individual

users each have virtual control of the shared memory. Pipelining is bought with a high redundancy of LSI firmware, for a great deal of "wired-in" instructions are called for to manage the traffic of concurrent executions.

The problem with these super systems, always present with computing, but magnified here by the size and the expectations size generates, may be largely administrative or procedural. Neither side, the manufacturer or the user, comes up with the software that's needed to take full advantage of the ramified storage and circuitry.

One of the greatest single computer systems—and, by most admissions, at rates exceeding 100 million instructions per second, the fastest—is ILLIAC IV. Truly a network in itself, consisting of a control unit and sixty-four "slave" computers, or processing elements, ILLIAC IV is but one node among many in shared networks such as ARPANET. (ARPANET consists of forty nodes and is sponsored by the Advanced Research Projects Agency of the Department of Defense.) Burroughs Corporation put together the subsystems for ILLIAC IV over a period of more than five years in a number of plants and had the whole thing ready for work at NASA/Ames, Moffett Field, California, in January 1973. One of the first users, and contributing much to the design, was the Center for Advanced Computation of the University of Illinois in Urbana.

In the design for ILLIAC IV, a single master control sends instructions to any number or all of the sixty-four processing elements and sends addresses to the corresponding memory units associated with them. In this way one program of instructions controls the execution cycles of all the processing elements, though they are each working on a different set of data. A problem of linear programming that would take a stand-alone large computer six to eight hours to solve could be done on ILLIAC IV in less than two minutes. This is the ultimate, it would seem, in parallel processing.

Though capable of acting in total unison, the individual elements have their own unique settings, and this is what allows them to operate in different ways at the same time.

The speed and multiplicity of operation actually give a different color, so to speak, to the calculations ILLIAC IV performs. Differential equations meant to define the temperature changes in a layer or layers of air—for purposes of predicting the weather—when handled in parallel rather than in series, afford a closer simulation of the actual physical process. For another thing, the speed of an array system like ILLIAC IV allows a far greater number of iterations than does a sequential operation within the same time. Thus the testing of a solution is more thorough, since more probabilities and variables have been looked over.

Tied into networks such as ARPANET, ILLIAC IV can supply rapid responses to problems relating to defense allocations. Similarly, in biology, it can readily sort out complex tangles of responses and conditions in areas of study like neurophysiology. The University of Illinois continues its now limited work with the system by running through ARPANET climate studies and a pattern-processing program for mapping the land resources of a region near the campus. In weather prediction, D. L. Slotnick of the University points out that ILLIAC IV has the potential to bring Goldstine's and von Neumann's ideal of fast numerical forecasting to closer realization, but in a way different from what they conceived. Rather than do a thirty-day forecast in the time—fifteen minutes in Goldstine's example—it takes to do twenty-four hours, Slotnick sees the system making predictions four times more detailed than at present, and because of that more accurate, in the same or less time. Stated another way, a five-day forecast with the accuracy of present forty-eight-hour forecasts, based on the quadrupled detail, can be done in the same computing time.

 Among the other very large systems that became

operational in the early seventies was the TI ASC, the Advanced Scientific Computer of Texas Instruments, Inc. It can transfer a maximum of 80 million words of data per second through each of its eight accessing units—an overall theoretical transfer rate of 640 million words per second. The time for an instruction to be carried out in central memory is 160 billionths of a second. One installation, out of six, is at the Institute for Advanced Study at Princeton conducting global weather forecasts.

Several others were STARAN, a series of associative array processors made by Goodyear Aerospace Corporation; MECL-20,000, reportedly under development by Motorola; and Honeywell's MULTICS.

It's a mistake to think that with all this building up of speeds and storage capacities, size is the goal, or even the only way to attain new levels in scientific calculations. It just happens that for specific uses, large integral systems like MULTICS or STARAN are best. The drive for compacting the process continues. And everything works in this direction. Nor does compactness work necessarily in favor of centralizing the processing function. The *Harvard Business Review* for May–June 1975 makes the case for decentralization for those who have found the large computers to be obstacles and encumbrances:

> . . . service levels seem to be deteriorating: users complain that data centers are lethargic and nonresponsive, and centralization of computer facilities all too often runs against the decentralized operations preferred by many companies.

The authors here, Gerald J. Burnett and Richard L. Nolan, encourage management to "think minis," to put the less expensive machines into the lower-level operating centers of their organizations.

Technology would seem to be on both sides, for, size apart, the trend indicates more and more interconnecting of all the nodes, components, processors, front-ends, whatever.

Whether in one package the size of a fat attaché case or filling a good part of a room and weighing seventy-five tons (ILLIAC IV), information will move, and the wiring of the world to bring this about will go forward. If for no other purpose than to handle the traffic, elaborate switching modules will be with us for some time. As demands for reliability and security grow with the spread of the networks, more elaborate equipment will be needed. Size may not increase, but complexity most certainly will.

So the machines are there, here, everywhere, and functioning at all hours: these networks, interchangeable chips and modules, terminals, front-ends, firmware. Business and management, and not just capitalistic, being what they are, the purveyors of the product are not always forthright with what is available, what technological twist is coming next. (They can't tip their hand, can't make "fighting machines" to drive out the competition, and yet they do it just the same.) And society fights its problems with an imperfect, robotic grasp of what superabundant means are at hand. Like the shoemaker's children, we go without shoes.

chapter 00101

Where Goes the Man?

I am a machine, nothing machine-like is alien to me.

Epitaph for late-twentieth-century man? Has the humanist dictum "I am a man, nothing human is alien to me" become twisted, irrelevant now to the possibilities and probabilities of the computer age? along with what it implied of pride in mankind (in oneself), of tolerance and understanding for others? We can't put numbers to values such as ease, contentment and beauty, so they're out of our calculations, alien to us. Possibilities and probabilities can be assigned numbers and can be processed; statistical presumptions too; they are in.

Spare the job and spoil the man

Labor unions are forced to collaborate with automation and the productivity engines that work toward the demise of all that unions have stood for—all, that is, that's beyond the next contract signing. They cave in "in the public interest," to "save the jobs . . . the company . . . the budget," as labor-saving data processing and equipment go onto the docks and into newspaper plants, steel mills, oil refineries, banks, insurance companies, utilities, government bureaus. They get what they can for the present members: attrition clauses, promises of transfers and retraining for the displaced, early pensions, company contributions to supplementary benefits that can be drawn on as long as the funds last in the case of recessionary layoffs. In real terms, in the interest of presently employed union members, and no others, they have surrendered to the computer hundreds of thousands of livelihoods. This is the true weight of disemployment: thousands of jobs made to totally disappear through attrition. And when the displaced are not members, or when their unions are weak or are captives of management, the major union leaders are known to be present only by the ego games they play with politics (Meany's support of Nixon in 1972), turning their backs on the forces of real reform.

Featherbedding everywhere and make-work schemes in government become the only achievable, if whispered, goals. As in the past—to save railroad firemen when there were no fires to tend in diesels, and typesetters when photocomposing machines were running their copy—featherbedding remains an impoverishing ransom for the hostages of progress. But to come down hard on the unions and the general myopia of labor, to the exclusion of all others, is dealing fast and loose with misplaced particulars. "The worker as commodity" was not the brainchild of the unions. Their misfortune, the unions', is that they have no other counters to play with.

The pace of job attrition quickens and can hardly be seen as slowing so long as the impulse toward miniaturization for a denser, more productive computing power for more automation for higher productivity continues. New plants aren't built and new ventures started with workers in mind. Labor-intensive industries become, for sheer survival, capital intensive; and numerical-control automation and process-control networks displace and disemploy untold thousands. Computers don't replace people or compete with them; people and numerical control (NC) machines are apples and oranges in the industrial shopping cart. The same "tasks" may be performed, but not the same "jobs," not really. Computers, it's been said, are faster, more efficient, safer, far cheaper, untiring; but more than any of this, they belong. Feeding the computer is a fail-safe algorithm, in the right kitchen, for success. Feeding the worker is chancy at best.

Richard M. Pfeffer observes in the *New York Times* (April 30, 1975):

> Profound economic crises expose how socio-economic systems operate. They strip away whatever niceties and humane concerns appear to be part of the normal operations of inhuman societies. The degree of exposure varies throughout the society. In such institutions as factories, where even under the best of conditions the system of hierarchical domination hardly appears humane, the impact of the present economic crisis has been immediate, the dehumanization total. . . .
>
> [Still, layoffs], as a particular kind of crisis [in any environment], dramatize issues embedded in normal work relations. Subordinates feel a one-sided dependency upon hierarchical power-holders and a consequent sense of individual helplessness that at times approaches terror.
>
> That subjective appreciation accurately reflects the objective treatment of workers as commodities in every sphere of production. . . . They are human commodities whose entire value lies in their capacity to produce by their labor whatever is defined as "productive" by the manipulated, interlocking markets.

The makings of revolution are not far from such insights. The honeymoon is over, if it ever began, between the computer and the industrial worker, and likewise the romance between middle managers and the new machines that have come into their lives. In place of, or added to, the revolution, the new disruptive attitude toward work could boil over into social chaos.

Challenges to the work ethic aren't observed only in columns in the *New York Times* and in unemployment lines, nor among graduating students facing tough competition for jobs. Brought up to heed admonitions like "labor is good in itself," still, few among us resist early and compensated retirement. More and more civil service people, policemen, whoever can, retire while still in their fifties, dropping out of "the rat race" in favor of a life of ease. People who work often take every opportunity to escape. Beyond that, an increasing number of Americans see no virtue in holding jobs that they consider menial or unpleasant. More and more reject them, even if they can get no other job. Even in periods of unemployment, it's well known that there are shortages of taxi drivers, domestics, auto mechanics and others.

A few enlightened employers have concluded that work, not the workers, must change. There are job enrichment programs meant to fit the person more comfortably into the industrial scheme, and there are some visionaries, not just in Sweden, who propose to: (1) treat workers like mature, responsible adults; (2) let groups of workers set their own schedules and manage their own work; (3) break up the assembly-line workers' jobs into varieties of tasks; and (4) let more workers take what part they can in the total operation, let them see the end product of their efforts.

Americans cling tenaciously to the puritanical belief that virtue will be rewarded, that success attends upon effort, that the poor are shiftless, and that it's their own fault they are poor. Ways of thinking change, however, and a more humane, more accurate view of poverty comes to the surface. The attitudes of the haves for the havenots is forever worthy of study if not summary dismissal.

Many hold steadfastly to Protestant and Old Testament beliefs and question the embrace by so many of negotiated, favorable early retirement. How can an able-bodied man, woman, *or* child not keep busy? how can anyone morally choose leisure over work? Latter-day puritans won't realize that to the extent that an individual curbs his enjoyment of the good things during his working life, saving for his retirement, early though it may be, he has actually made his contribution. They won't see that each retiring worker reduces not a jot of the potential output, the total amount of goods and services available for total consumption.

With life expectancy increasing and the population maturing, it might be prudent for society to rethink some of these notions. Rather than consuming what he's not producing, the person retired from the work force is contributing to production. He's releasing the residue of what he's earned (and held back, or had held back for him) during his working years. Such a one is no less deserving of respect than those who stay on producing. Programmed leisure or leisure forced on one by unemployment does not result in a smaller pie to be sliced up among the constituents of an economy. The work is there to be done and will be done.

We are afraid, it appears, not to work because unemployment makes us look helpless in the eyes of our neighbors. The seeming craving for work also aggravates the anguish of aging. Unfortunately for most, the only reality one has to adapt to is the job he has at the moment, and when one has aged, he feels "left out." Society and the students of society have not designed anything useful for one to do that suits the lessening capacities of old age. They find it simpler to pension one off or to ignore him. Mixed up though one's life may be, one learns to like working. Few concerns of modern man are as poignant and as lingering as the threat and eventual blow of unemployment. Who will work and who won't? Who will know where to apply and where not?

That soon most of the demeaning, dirty, routine and boring jobs will be done automatically is no longer the pipe dream or paranoid nightmare it once was. What's more, the usual entrées to jobs—the union card, the diploma, the connections—no longer pay off as they once did in blue-collar, white-collar, and management positions.

People with active imaginations and hungry intellects—sociologists, scientists, teachers, artists, the synthesizers and the analysts, medical researchers, and people trained in fields hardly yet thought of or not thought of at all—will do the work of tomorrow. But what happens to those who in spirit will always belong to the precomputer age? What happens to those, perhaps the majority, who are incapable of attaching themselves to the cybernetic loop, of being scientists or artists, who haven't the scope of curiosity or aren't bright enough to qualify for a secure place in the new society? They might find as time goes on that we're underestimating them. Some may be far less limited than we suspect. Education and a changed perspective can do wonderful work on people who have been written off as untrainable and unteachable.

C. P. Snow, novelist and scientist, author of *The Two Cultures*, has commented extensively on the effect of the new technology on culture. In *Computers and Automation* (April 1966) he states that the answer to the psychological disadvantages of the "technological tide" is to see that men are not submerged in it.

> In practical terms [he goes on], a great many operations will be done by computers which are now being done by men. We've got to foresee this long before it happens. If we have the foresight and the technological skills, most of those practical effects—the nonpsychological effects—can probably be at least mollified and, to some extent, wiped away. But there is a long-term effect for which I see very little answer. It looks as though once you firmly establish a society advanced in this cybernetic way, then ten or perhaps twenty percent of the population will have to work

extremely hard. Men of the whole managerial slice of society will have more tasks, more difficult and more complicated, than they've ever had before. On the other hand, it seems to me inescapable that a large slice of the population, perhaps as much as eighty percent, will be underemployed, and will remain underemployed for the next hundred years or so; but in the long run, in a really advanced society, I can't see any easy way out from this. People will in fact cease to have an ethic based on work; they are bound to have an ethic based very largely on non-work. This is worrying me, but it has great advantages. If I had to choose, I'd take it, because most men who ever lived, the overwhelming majority of our fellow human beings, have in fact lived lives which were short and hideous to contemplate; they worked from the cradle to the grave, with extraordinarily little compensation. This has been the ordinary lot of man from time immemorial. And so, therefore, to take that burden away is fine, and I'll settle for that.

The choice is being made for us. The costs of the thinking and doing machines continue to plunge; they become increasingly cost-effective, "cost-justifiable," and this means that jobs are threatened whenever people are paid more than the cost of machines doing the same or similar work. And it means unmanageable unemployment.

There are those, thoughtful people, who see in this the prospect of nothing but an avalanche, the worst calamity ever. The recession-inflation of the mid-seventies turns people's minds to the thirties—to not-so-nostalgic visions of the able-bodied, the strong-willed and the experienced, reduced to total defeat, of families and communities, whole cities, losing possessions, comfort and traditions that they've struggled lifetimes and generations to acquire.

The walking source of error

William E. Zisch made the crack: "Individualism is being gobbled up by huge computers; they turn each of us into a giant IBM card that differs from the real ones only in the placement of the holes." The economist Robert Theobald, as quoted in *Life* (August 14, 1964), has said:

> Compared to a functionally neat, clean, odorless, efficiently and continuously functioning cybernetic machine system, a unit of mankind is messy, soiled, smelly, disobedient, quarrelsome, lazy and a walking source of error. For those . . . already in a state of emotional and sensory atrophy, a machine is easier to go with than a man. Inevitably, the number of people capable of competing with machines will decline and the unemployed will increase.

The obsoleting of skills and products, and whole industries and institutions, would be topics for barbershop bull sessions were barbershops still the community centers they once were. People are left to regroup and restructure their skills because jobs have to be kept or other jobs found.

Engineers, accountants, teachers aren't alone: so many people are dismayed by the intense pressures on them to keep current, to spend free nights in classes for the rest of their careers, just to keep up. Companies and organizations, if they're seriously committed to maintaining loyalty, performance and spirit among their people, recognize their duty in this and contribute time and funds to the efforts at self-help. Periodic retraining and sabbaticals of from six months to two years can easily be foreseen. As it is, few organizations seem able to look beyond immediate demands and to start such programs. Certain specialists take the position that industry programs must enable an employee to spend one workday a week in craft or vocational schools, colleges, universities or company courses. Attacking symptoms, however, and not the disease, if that's what the eco-spasm is, relieves pain and sustains life only after a fashion. It's important to remember that at the root of it all is policy and the structuring of attitudes, wherever that has its source, and not technology and the computer.

Anyone two years into a career knows that jobs live or

die on one's contribution or not to earnings. Times of economic stress drive managers to drive for greater and greater efficiency: the success or failure of ruthless efforts at cost control on the manager's part will save or destroy his own job. Controlling costs requires vigorous, continuing efforts. There are expenses that can't be eliminated. Still, every unneeded and unwanted, redundant and wasted expenditure of time, effort, material, money is fair game for a scrubbing under the relentless, unpitying scan of the computer. Time and experience prove the computer an excellent "judge" of employee nonfulfillment. Process control, sensibly handled, boosts the efficiency of every employee and machine, with the result that automation fosters automation. To all the well-known factors—nothing succeeding like success, growing sophistication about the machines, lower costs, tax breaks for capital expenses—add inflation. It makes the computer and its advocates look really good. Wage increases bring on the famous profit squeeze, and that forces the manager to act *against* people and *for* smart machines.

But people are not capital, one is excited to shout. It didn't take the Communist Manifesto or Lincoln's Emancipation Proclamation to establish that. A company can invest in people, in their careers, in their futures, but it cannot *buy* them. Whatever reverse comfort lies in the notion of the wage slave or the worker as commodity, people cannot be owned, except figuratively or by default of conscience on one side or the other. Machines can be owned, are owned and have to be. Because investment in machinery displaces money paid to people at no sacrifice to output, the system has to prefer, where the choice is open, to own the more efficient means rather than to hire the chancy, not tradable factor, and the displaced people, as things stand, have their freedom to scrabble for themselves.

Inside or outside employment, the degradation can be total. The robots, NC machines, process and systems control set a nasty pace, "burn a man up" in ten years. However, to put only young men to work under these conditions can be, as they say, counterproductive. The under-thirties at Lordstown proved that in 1972. They might have had the bodies to stand the strain but they hadn't the stupidity. It's true, there are peak years for every skill. Mathematicians, like poets and musicians, have been known to do their most brilliant before reaching twenty-five. Female swimmers seem in their prime under sixteen. And, with peak years past, there can remain some pretty high plateaus. Kinsey said the American male is best sexually at fourteen and the female at thirty-two. Life goes on.

And job profiles are written, and rewritten, to best effectuate the tightrope between expendable, firable, rehirable, transferable man and high-capital computer equipment. Past certain peaks, workers are programmed into retraining and transfers. Elimination and downgrading are no news to many over fifty. Their reactions prove too slow. Computer-aided design with interactive graphics is said to increase the decision-making power of the engineer or the architect by a factor of seventy. The question in such instances has to be: How many decisions can one draftsman, engineer or architect make? Still, the threat is there; the more productive the individual, the fewer individuals in like jobs there have to be.

Knowledge, an individual's knowledge, especially of modern technology and the computer, tends to obsolesce. A famous equation: the technological advances of the last twenty-five years are equal to or greater than all those before. A book like Rein Turn's *Computers in the 1980s* is hardly printed and bound before the author's projections into the eighties for improvements in the speeds, for instance, of nonimpact printers are exceeded in 1975 in IBM's model 3800 by a factor of ten. And this is not to the forecaster's discredit. "The speed of technological advance," an editorial by Norman A. McRae in *The Economist* (January 1972) states, "has been so tremendous during the past decade that the useful life of knowledge of many of those trained to use computers has been about three years."

Those who might be successful enough to reach a fairly high-level job by the time they're thirty often find themselves so busy they can't take the time or leave to update themselves. Without dedicated study or some form of retreading, the best people fall behind. By the time they're sixty, *The Economist* observes, they have no more than an eighth the grip they ought to have on management, science and technology. The competition of machines, or of men better informed about the machines, would, long before that, have likely overtaken and disemployed them. The stress this places upon staff workers, particularly older men, can't be overestimated. Downward mobility, demoralization, destructive habits like drinking, physical and mental deterioration too often go with such a career. A union matter or not, there are institutional responsibilities here: the right of people at any age to work at a civilized tempo; the right to technological upgrading through education at company or public expense on company time.

However, these problems which are restricted to the elite, well-trained minority of the work force are dwarfed in comparison to the plight of workers on the assembly lines and at the work stations of giant corporations and mass-producing industries.

The modern, productivity-driven corporation or industrial conglomerate is a hard case. Worker and union demands for decent working conditions are, as often as not, met with the threat that relocation can always move the enterprise to a more congenial labor source in another region, or, in the case of the multinational corporation, to another country. And maybe it's not even a threat, but a fait accompli.

Cutting the mustard—on the line

Faced with the steady march of automation, computerization and cybernation into their plants and factories, particularly onerous to workers, bugging them like nothing else, are CPM and PERT—critical path method and program evaluation and review technique (pages 44–45). With PERT in force, each worker is evaluated, online and instantly. The computers draw on past experiences to determine, among other things, performance times and the amounts and costs of normal or substitutable resources. The programs determine whether a standard or unacceptable pace is being maintained at every work station. One of the techniques is exception reporting—flashing reports of every unplanned or abnormal event to remote "bosses"—computerized or in the flesh.

Computers have changed many things since the days of time-motion studies. Computers are very efficient in measuring, testing, and scheduling. Supervisors of production are alerted, simultaneously and automatically, when any one worker is not producing at least his average established quota of events. For example, General Motors feeds time-study data from all its far-flung plants into computers. The computers then catalog the readings, break every job and job section down into discrete elements of work, and then report the labor allotment based on these inputs. Irving Bluestone, Vice President of the United Automobile Workers in charge of GM affairs, complains, "The robot says to the worker, given these elements, this is how much time you have to do it." He further complains that the computer pits one plant against another, and thereby pressures the managers, who in turn pressure the workers, causing some jobs to have unrealistically tight time allotments. Management counters with the "system facts," that the time studies are based on thousands of readings and accurately assess the time required for each job and job segment. If some people can't "cut the mustard," they must go.

Executives and stockholders can't fault these programs. Nor can union leaders effectively fight them. The efficiency engine reigns supreme where either is concerned. Expensive behavioral scientists show managers new approaches that meet the approval of those who pay for their studies but not of the workers. Needless to say, they're not consulted.

Union leaders find themselves forced to agree to principles like: To produce more with the same amount of human effort is a sound economic and social objective. Most also concede that job-cutting is legitimate, with the demur that the methods aren't so nice—the merging of departments, the rotating of hard-driving foremen. Managers who don't "innovate" in the interest of productivity are firing themselves, taking a critical path to the dustbin.

A complaint: They pulled manpower out of all the plants, the body shop, the paint shop and they pulled ten out of nineteen people in the headlining department, forcing nine men to do the same work as nineteen because they said the job was light (overmanned).

One man's job was to install two bolts on the bumper of the cars coming down the assembly line "65 seconds apart." But computer time studies alerted his supervisors that the job was light. They eliminated the man across from him and instructed him to install from then on four bolts on each car, as well as to replenish his own stock, this latter a new task. In effect, the work for this job was more than doubled, and if he fought it by saying he was unable to keep up, he was out.

With it all comes the discipline of machine systems, imposing minute-by-minute control over workers, and from their side, the workers' outrage muffled by the fiercely competitive need to hold one's job at any cost and under any condition. What else is either management or labor to do but cope under the circumstances and think productivity?

Whatever the outcome, however workable means are devised to humanize "the system" as it grows in automation and information transfer, the major problem would seem to be: How to distribute the abundance cybernation creates without regard to individual contributions, and to let profits and increases in production, consumption, and income follow upon that. With the consumer as the real judge of merit, as he has not been since the earliest craft guilds, and as he's supposed to be if the free market system and advertising have any meaning, we'd have a true restructuring of the social order. Without pay, what's more, as the full incentive for work, we'd go into a true seller's market in matters of hiring and job-seeking.

No one ought to be surprised: Computerization, altering attitudes and relationships—indeed furnishing the links to supranational networks—begs that ethical and political tests be applied. Humanists are bound to devise matrices of hitherto unquantified considerations.

These machines that take less than a generation to increase themselves and multiply, that invent other machines, systems, programs and processes, the Turing machine in the tens of thousands winding out the tapes of its own simulations and perpetuity—never mind that they are not self-aware, that their intelligence is artificial. There's so little of the genuine article elsewhere that they have an easy time.

Marya Mannes said on a TV talk show long ago that when someone tried to compliment her with "You think like a man," she would answer, "Which man?"—a remark a computer might well hold in storage for a like exchange.

Computers, unlike man, lack imagination, it's said. What's imaginative about a Lordstown? What's creative about responding to a hypothetical and induced "strangulation" by the oil-producing nations with threats of nuclear retaliation?

Isn't it really the case that we are protecting the machinery that's used in our growth-oriented society rather than the people who are supposed to use it and purchase its output? Inhumanity, like crime, pays, and goes undetected even by the perpetrator, if we let it. Stress under the pressure of inhuman goals will grow, if we let it. There will be efforts at correction and control. Specific goals will be set. Unions and management will in turn propose and reject them, reject and propose: shorter workweeks, longer holidays, more paid education, and greater amounts of leisure time with some structure and not just idle and free escape. Many believe that twenty-eight-hour workweeks or even shorter ones are not only desirable, but indeed imperative. Other, more general goals suggest themselves, like the encouragement of people to take a nonsentimental but consistent and real look at their obligations toward others.

There are the makings of a politics in all this, but it is hard to see what and who will turn them into shape. Writing about the lessons to be drawn from the Vietnam War, Susan Sontag says, "The [Peace] Movement was never sufficiently political; its understanding was primarily moral; and it took considerable moral vanity to expect that one could defeat the considerations of *Realpolitik* mainly by appealing to considerations of 'right' and 'justice.' " (*New York Review of Books*, June 12, 1975) There are, she suggests, citing Thucydides, some eternal actualities one might better seize in the face of horrible events and at times of crisis.

Industrial fragmentation has always meant that jobs are broken down into narrow definitions of skills. It's a fragmentation common to virtually all pursuits and professions —whether industrial or not. People everywhere become distinct segments of systems. They are components. They are "specified"—in job profiles—like materials and instruments. Each skill is defined within the parameters of a system. And as technology's complexity grows, each of the functions is fragmented into ever narrower, more specialized units. The new capital-intensive processing forms neat, inelastic niches for elastic man to be squeezed into.

Experience and tests have shown that the more you give some people to do, the more specialized the demands you put to them, the more they *give,* the more they stretch. It's also well known that the properties of materials have limits, and when a material or a person is stretched beyond the maximum of elasticity, it (or he) snaps. Fragged, you might say. Whence, in factory or office, the growing number of nervous disorders and neuroses, and, perhaps more insidious because it's unconscious and self-protective, or robotic, the shying away from decency.

Computer talk, especially having to do with microprocessors and minicomputers, is rife with references to *dedicated* machines. Job definitions grind out dedicated "appendages" to the machine—the input operator, for instance; the output user. Our educational system is being distorted to produce an overstock of these narrowly dedicated, and redundant, specialists. Thinking, most places, has little to do with the processes of education. What have narrow, dedicated skills to do with thinking? How better to keep people content within the oubliettes of job function? What point the overview? Overall goals and purpose don't have to exist if they can't be thought of or put into readable, speakable form. Education for compassion and caring has little to do with the fabrication of dual-inline packages (DIPs). And dedicated DIPs know their function. Don't ask a zigger to zag. Don't ask a semiconductor manufacturer why microprocessors are still five years at best from a consumer-oriented use in cars, and don't ask a major source of information or a mainframe marketer why home terminals for computer access are still in a hopeless snarl of unattached components. To the question, "What active efforts does your organization have to cope with the 'dehumanizing' image of the computer?" IBM answered, in *Computers and People* (March 1975): "The future of technology in the United States is being shaped less in industrial plants and laboratories than it is in the classroom and library and quiet places of humane learning."

In simple fact, the computer is an extension of man. It's not hard to postulate that man willed an extension of his eyes and so invented the telescope and the microscope; he willed even greater visual power and invented radar, the electron microscope and the radio telescope. He extended muscle and limb through hydraulic and pneumatic power; his energy through the harnessing of steam, electricity, the cracked or fused atom, heat and the sun's rays. Has he now willed the extension of memory, cognition, deduction, induction through the computer? Has he willed a consistent, rational, manipulable framework for his powers of judgment? We think because the machine is, or is it that the machine is because we think?

Computer specialists are not necessarily the only ones to use their skills and ingenuity to create all this technological change. Anyone can invent a program—that is, a system, a new tool, or another invented machine, or a process that takes the place of one.

Man has the power if he'll use it to exploit these new media of skill and ingenuity. With them he can prepare the ground for a fuller and more dignified existence. These drives into untraveled lands are exciting, yet they can be seen to be narrowing the margins of freedom. It's a narrowing and fading that could be terminal. Is it a power then to be welcomed, or to be left to drift, unorganized, or organized for the parochial gains of the hydras of power, those supranational elites of untouchable privilege? It's not the business of such elites to guarantee some populist prosperity. Nor is it their business to disabuse us of the myths of progress. The blind, unthinking drive of technology only seems to be taking us forward. It could instead be wreaking irrecoverable losses, to the environment, to our liberties, our communities, our nations. Patriotism, once the refuge of scoundrels, could become, under the reckless adventurism of multinational corporations, the last prayer of the hopeless. As for the computer, it cannot of itself make sure that technology serve the interests of all the people and not be used to maximize profit and productivity alone.

Profit might have to be made redundant, not the human components who produce it. Useful when it's present, profit is not the be-all and end-all. Lockheed and the Penn Central aren't the only inefficient, yet essential, systems to be saved from insolvency, from their own ineptitude. There are no sacred standards by which failure can be graded, one institution or person deserving of salvation, another not. An individual employee's inability to adapt to a certain productivity loop is not in itself to be taken as a passport to oblivion.

However, the time is near when *man-hours* will be a meaningless measure of output. Forced leisure, in its various guises, will enlarge the educational system and shift its emphasis toward the arts of "personal growth," and the rebirth of the ancient Greek attitudes toward work and life. "There's more to life than just working, and more to working than just working for some company," an unemployed certified public accountant told a *New York Times* reporter in the spring of 1975.

> How many other Americans hold similar views is impossible to measure [the article goes on], though the group [of job dropouts] is considered atypical of the 8.2 million people officially classified as unemployed. But at a time when the nation is experiencing its highest rate of unemployment in more than 25 years, it is apparent from recent interviews in eight cities that there are many middle-class Americans who are not working because they choose not to and many others who are being very selective in accepting a job before surrendering their unemployment status.

The recession, by making jobs harder to get, has made being out of work more socially acceptable. By stimulating Government action to extend unemployment benefits, it has made survival easier.

Discouraged workers, the dropouts among the unemployed, were estimated, at the time of the *Times* article, to number just over a million. Even were they not disenchanted with the work ethic, they'd not have been able, according to experts, to find jobs in the recession. Even more, it's doubtful that a return to good times would change their outlook or improve the prospect. No one's talking about automation in the *Times*'s report, but it's there. Among the responses were things like:

But I don't feel people should have to work for the profit of other people. . . . Work is the opiate of the masses. If you must work for something, it's not worth having. I don't believe in things—possessions. There are only two kinds of people who are happy—those who have so much that no matter how much is taken from them, they still have plenty, and those who don't have anything. Those in the middle are the unhappy ones. That's why I say: Don't work, enjoy life.

Monks at the time of Abelard and Heloise suffered from accidie, "one of the seven chief sins," according to *The Middle Ages: 395–1500* by Joseph R. Strayer and Dana C. Munro.

There is no modern equivalent for the word [we further learn]; it was an acute form of boredom, a feeling that life was useless and dreary. It might result merely in laziness and distaste for monastic duties, or it might—and frequently did—lead to suicide. In its milder forms it caused monks to invent excuses for journeys and changes of occupation—some went to study at Paris, others to visit a shrine, others to visit sick kinsmen. Some of these wandering monks never returned, and their life became a scandal to the moralists.

It's easy to see that for those who now thrive on work, finding substitutes for the ethical discipline of work, as the cybernetic age evolves, will be psychologically painful, far more so than the crisis of adjusting to a second or third car.

The unemployment problem in 1980 should be, in the language of *Clockwork Orange*, statistically "horror-show." Spread-the-work expedients can hardly succeed up to expectations: automation, we won't forget, adds no jobs; it subtracts them, it destroys jobs. The rate of job destruction and the net loss, or gain, in human-to-machine productivity will be subject to much dispute. Experts, even today, can't agree on the rates of technological unemployment.

So far not part of any calculations are the real costs to the community of the self-destroying, drinking, depressed or on-drugs dropouts from the system—the accidie sufferers of our day. Yet affirmative-acting and public service outlays to community programs are put forth as signs of corporate enlightenment and liberality. They are gestures without the hint of an admission that the industrial milieu sets the preconditions for the self-destruction.

In the past, before industry imposed its lock-step rules, people had moral supports that helped them endure toil, hardship and suffering. The work ethic, becoming ever less hallowed, once included religious faith, and it sustained frameworks of tradition and custom, a sense of place in the order of things, a sense of worth derived from the exercise of craftsmanship, and an awareness that toil, hardship and suffering were likewise endured by other members of the same community and the same social class.

Science, the bulwark of technology, attacks faith and certainty. It leaves every last member of society on his own, out for himself and his, or at least feeling that way. Hence the "flash crises" of social uproar—decent people turned into monsters over school busing. For all of an enlightened management's efforts to accommodate people to the machine and vice versa, the introduction of automated procedures only sharpens the sense of insecurity. People are motivated not to be motivated.

Uncertainty on a world scale, change upon change, fierce business competition that crosses industrial and national borders, the adversary relationship unrelenting everywhere, "bad" attitudes toward work and authority, authoritarian overreaction, universal bloody-mindedness, leave few comforts to a troubled soul. And there's that old stand-by, inflation. Inflation has already caused full employment to be impossible by pricing millions of consumers out of many markets—cars, to begin with. Little but piecemeal reaction has come from the major governments.

Automation is a way in and a way out of the muddle. How it will be handled will have much to do with balancing out the conflicting forces at work. "Intelligent factories" are already at a stage of growth in Western Europe and Japan that American unions might never allow factories in the U.S. to achieve. Automated techniques stimulate massive demands—for the throwaway lighters, for instance, and the under-thirty-dollar electronic calculator, not to mention the transistor radio, a virtual appendage on the "mean streets" of the world. Industrial nations, as well as the resource-rich Third World nations, must all force the products of automation into world markets to make any sense of their export-import balances. The effects of automation become ever more unpredictable. Disemployment and inflation seem not to be confinable. An economically beset United States cuts its imports and thereby shuts down factories and brings deficits to the healthiest of trading partners.

In all the scurry, there's the scandal of "administered costs" and "whipsaw prices"—as variously termed accounting tricks that include artificial setups of nonexistent costs, false reserves, the playing off of one country's tax laws against another's, prices bearing no relation to costs or to supply and demand but as agreed to among controlling, interested groups—the multinationals, the international banking firms.

Many people don't understand the computer's role. They don't trust it, or they believe it to be only a tool or a servant. To them it has a life of its own, an energy and an initiative independent of man, in competition with man. They see it little by little dispossessing the human being from his divinely ordained summit in the animal kingdom, robbing him of a job and a living, depriving him of a reason for being—of a place to go every morning at nine. They've seen the automatic dishwasher and the automatic shoeshine kit, the automatic assembly line and the automatic accounting machine. They know there's more to come, and that sooner or later no occupation and no skill will be safe from the machine's supposed depredations. People also know that computers will be used in dangerous areas, like aversion therapy, where serious philosophical questions arise: How far may science be allowed to go in the conditioning of living creatures? Antivivisectionists aren't alone in doubting the validity of research that accepts the torturing of animals, let alone "marginal" humans—prisoners, mental patients, the retarded, the institutionalized of any sort—the near perfect biometric sample. And what about the military uses of computers, sensors, automatons and cybernetics? It is estimated that from 10 to 15 percent of the total EDP output (more than $20 billion) in America goes into war-related activities of the federal government. It's no wonder that the computer is feared as the ultimate and most terrifying development of the technological age. It's a master, and an enemy.

Man has always feared the machine and science and the progress they represent. He has fought innovation even when it has demonstrably made life more endurable. Innovation means change. It brings chaos and confusion. It's inconvenient. It arouses curiosity and casts doubt on grounds that had been certain, calls traditions and custom into question. It ravels the carefully woven fabric of our lives. Innovation lights up the dark corners of the mind. It makes us think; it's hateful.

Hostility to change is not limited to those whose jobs are most immediately at stake. People oppose change in all honesty, out of idealism and compassion. They see it robbing man of his self-respect, his human qualities, and turning him, too, into a monster. They can't believe that man is capable of holding his own in a contest with the cold, inflexible rationality of a machine. They see man going into spiritual exile, and the graceless machine inheriting the earth.

Weird thing to say, these beliefs are right, the more widely and firmly they're held. The computer does take on a life and force of its own, the more restricted is the access to it—the more remote its control from the democratic base. So, what to do? Everyone his own programmer? You have nothing to lose but your own ignorance? Only with a hands-on, working experience with a computer can one begin to weigh its true and great worth, as an instrument more powerful than anything ever before in the hands of man.

According to Robert S. Lee, the social psychologist:

> In the long run, it will probably be the youngsters who grow up in a world of computers who will more truly understand the new relationship of man and the machine. They will not be handicapped by older concepts; they will not feel a sense of ego threat and they will not be in some sort of identity crisis in relation to machines. Instead, I believe they will be eager to understand the new tools, to use them to extend their knowledge and to extend their freedom to build the kind of future they want. And, out of this, I think a new concept of man will develop—a concept of man which includes and accepts his ability to amplify the powers of his mind . . .

Here we come full circle back to our starting point: Information is power. With it one can command great resources; without it one can command nothing and is rather a resource oneself to be commanded by others. Information is the millennial litmus that divides the classes of society, the haves from the havenots, as Galbraith has said education does, and as, before our time, money, property, birth had done in their turn.

Political and financial competition for the possession and control of information is apparent and intense. The collecting, processing and moving of information have great effects on the setting of policy, with real elitist forces at work, controlling information and capable of conscienceless manipulations of people.

Files on American dissidents from the days of the Peace Movement, files which the Justice Department had agreed to destroy in 1971 as a result of exposure by Senator Sam Ervin's committee, have a way of reappearing, in first one data bank of the Army or the CIA or the FBI and then another. As NBC News reported in early June 1975, a run of names, numbers, political affiliations and activities was transferred from one government data bank and run on computers at MIT: denials all around; suspicions of maneuverings by proto-thought police.

Organizations no longer work under the direction of a single individual. Interlocking staffs, committees, study groups, task forces determine and execute policy. Enter the computer and the means of "polling the experts," and responsibility is diffused. To cite Rein Turn once again:

> The Delphi method was developed at The Rand Corporation in 1964 . . . for both normative and exploratory long-range forecasting (i.e., into the twenty-first century). It is characterized by three features which distinguish it from other consensus-achieving group forecasts . . . :
>
> * *Anonymity.* The group members are not known to each other, and all interactions are handled in anonymous fashion; hence the undue influence of prominent group members can be eliminated and ideas can be assessed on their own merits only. A certain pressure to conform with the group consensus remains, however.

* *Interaction with controlled feedback.* The group members are kept informed of the current consensus, but are not harassed by arguments over their views. Majority and minority opinions can be maintained but will not overwhelm each other through the intensity and frequency of presentations or prominence of the partisans.
* *Statistical group response.* The distribution of the opinions of all participants can be presented and statistically analyzed (if expressed in an analyzable way).

These features are greatly enhanced by utilizing computer programs which can immediately score the participant's input against the current consensus, as well as update the consensus itself. The computer provides an effective means of enforcing anonymity and providing the controlled feedback. Remote access through remote terminals increases the convenience and speed of running the Delphi exercise.

Following the Rand paradigm to the letter or adapting it to decision-making by committee and computer, at any level we succeed in limiting the responsibility of the individual. As John Ehrlichman so tellingly etched the notion into the public consciousness, let the other guy—in this instance L. Patrick Gray III—not him, nor the President and his men, "hang there. Let him twist slowly, slowly in the wind." Hannah Arendt said in *Crises of the Republic* (1972):

> Today we ought to add the latest and perhaps most formidable form of . . . domination: bureaucracy or the rule of an intricate system of bureaus in which no men, neither one nor the best, neither the few nor the many, can be held responsible, and which could be properly called rule by Nobody. (If, in accord with traditional political thought, we identify tyranny as government that is not held to give account of itself, rule by Nobody is clearly the most tyrannical of all, since there is no one left who could even be asked to answer for what is being done. It is this state of affairs, making it impossible to localize responsibility and to identify the enemy, that is among the most potent causes of the current world-wide rebellious unrest, its chaotic nature, and its dangerous tendency to get out of control and to run amuck.)

Again, in Arendt's words, "Where all are guilty, no one is;

confessions of collective guilt are the best possible safeguard against the discovery of culprits, and the very magnitude of the crime the best excuse for doing nothing."

Many good people escape into the structure of an organization or into an elite perfectionism. Others drop out or take a mental powder. They lose interest and their commitment. One avoids "being involved" and easily falls into white-collar crime and the "diseases" of alienation. On the fringe, or apparently on the fringe, are overt hostility and dissidence, organizing into antisystem groups both inside and outside the organization. Those who "make it" use their elitist positions and organizational "clout" to capture some of the best qualified "Prussians," technicians with a high loyalty quotient. Identity is thus buried in "secret team" loyalties. Instead of dropping out, the elitist gives himself body and soul to the team. Knowing well the limited power of the individual, the team loyalist invests heavily in the highly disciplined power of the group and, beyond that, of the organization. Needing scapegoats when things go wrong, he has little pain finding them in rival groups or organizations or among the social misfits and outcasts. Perhaps this is what defeated the Watergate coverup: Nixon and his men, confronted with the law, were unable, try as they might, to remain anonymous. When it works, however, elitism allows the individual to shut himself off from and repress his own integrity and moral sense.

Needless to say, the computer in the hands of such elites is working, only by accident, if at all, in the public interest. The dealings in pooled projections, the turning of these projections into actualities that can work as barriers to programs, traps to ensnare ideas and points of view alien to the system, put a tight clamp, in effect, on all computers. The systems, finally, are made for the spectral elites. The procurement lists of the bureaucracies and the purchases of the giant corporations set systems specifications and procedural formats—the architecture of the mainframes, the configurations of firmware and the networks, the global library of software. The Tyranny of Nobody obsolesces old ideas of censorship. In computers, censorship, the tailoring of information, is mandatory. Computers, in the hands of isolated "committees of public safety," fashion information to preordained ends. This is not demonology: computers aren't bad, but the managers of them are when they are isolated, by force of circumstance, from their own and from accepted rules of conduct.

Information, then, is managed. So are the inferences and judgments derived from it and all or whatever part of behavior derived from that information, shaped and swayed by it. Creativity and intuition too fit into the scheme or find no scope. The very controls, of access principally, to the machines and the information they contain are subverted. Rather than protection, the public gets control, control of itself. The right to know becomes Nobody's right, as does the right to privacy.

Where Nobody reigns, the Dr. Strangelove goings on in matters military, especially in Southeast Asia, remain shocking but not unlikely in retrospect. The automated battlefield, a brainchild of the Institute of Defense Analysis, is the logical outcome of the many secret systems studies there were rumors about in the sixties. A simple definition of the automated battlefield is not possible. Equipment ranges from antipersonnel mines and laser-guided bombs to sensors that record odors (emitted by humans and monkeys), sounds (footsteps magnified when button bombs are stepped on), body heat, and voices. Information from the sensors was relayed during the war to computer centers in Cambodia, Laos and Thailand, where it was analyzed and appropriate orders, usually calling in ground or air fire, were given. Drone aircraft were added to the collective punch. With no pilot or crew, there'd be no "nervous nellies" to refuse a mission. The military may have reached the point where the blame for the My Lais of the future could be laid to "computer error." Nobody again.

Over these elites and their shadow controls there have been victories. Two presidents who were found wanting in candor—Lyndon B. Johnson and Richard M. Nixon—found themselves helped from office by one form or another of public activism. GM was not alone in feeling the lash of Ralph Nader and the consumerist fires his ardor ignited. Demands for more truth in advertising, more safety in product design, more self-fulfillment in jobs, better environmental controls, security from unconscionable surveillance are consistent with the dynamism of today's society. There will always be demands that are unreasonable. But it is one task of ethics to distinguish between reasonable and unreasonable standards, and another to shape institutions that will sustain the reasonable. Businessmen are being forced to resist the impulse to turn their backs on the rising tide of moral criticism while they "get on with the job" of producing goods and services. Adverse public views now deeply penetrate the total corporate system itself. There's often a connection between morality and morale, and a managerial group riddled by doubts of its own moral health might lose the internal trust that its vigor largely depends upon.

And putting on a moral face is not enough. With alert consumerism, pressures and needs inside and outside the organization force management to work up a conscious, systematic interest in ethical questions. Commercial motivations will have to be brought into a much clearer relationship with consumer demands. Business must behave better to exist. Business is subject too to all ethical constraints, including the plainest ones.

Somewhere, somehow, business and much of society must be thrown back upon what might be called "barefoot morality." This is the rich and indispensable resource that everyone but the psychopath has inherited. It's the ability to tell right from wrong in most situations of everyday life. Barefoot morality is as clear and pertinent to business as it is to you and me. Barefoot morality embraces broad ethical principles such as honesty, the obligation to tell the truth, to oneself, to one's fellow man, and to one's children.

A program

The discussion leads, it's to be hoped, to the care reasonable men (and machines) must take in the way they use, restrict yet broaden, and control the powers and capabilities of machine computation. Above all, the ongoing information can be one of our greatest blessings, or it can be the beginning of a terrible and irreversible tyranny.

Technology has presented man with benefits and comforts aplenty. Practical, working computers have been with us, unbelievably, for only twenty years. But now, married to communications, education, commerce, manufacturing, other technologies and government, they very suddenly have pitched society into manifold crises of direction and decision. Society is given no leave to adapt, to study, analyze, and prepare for what becomes unalterable change before it settles in (racing the moving target). The sudden, increased pace of change, its great pervasiveness, the diversity and versatility of computer performance and power, excite protest—for all the vanity and inappropriateness of the gesture—against the too many and too grave problems that too soon are thrust upon us.

The computer excels all others, outdoes all else as an instrument of control. Can this power be preserved as a staying force for the good of everyone, or will it continue to be stolen and withheld by an elite of scientists, militarists, bureaucrats and information entrepreneurs? According to Hannah Arendt:

> The enormous growth of productivity in the modern world was by no means due to an increase in the workers' productivity, but exclusively the development of technology, and this depended neither on the working class nor on the bourgeoisie, but on the scientists. The "intellectuals" . . . suddenly ceased to be a marginal social group and emerged as a new elite, whose work, having changed the conditions of human life almost beyond recognition in a few decades, has remained essential for the functioning of society. There are many reasons why this new group has not, or not yet, developed into a power elite, but there is indeed every reason to believe Daniel Bell [in "Notes on the Post-Industrial Society," *The Public Interest*, No. 6, 1967] that "not only the best talents, but eventually the entire complex of social prestige and social status, will be rooted in the intellectual and scientific communities." . . . For better or worse—and I think there is every reason to be fearful as well as hopeful—the really new and potentially revolutionary class in society will consist of intellectuals, and their potential power, as yet unrealized, is very great, perhaps too great for the good of mankind.

The unforeseen abuse, and the possibility of abuse, of computer controls—having to do with money, privacy, employment, communications, education, our Bill of Rights and heritage of individualism and freedom—are causing resentment and outright antagonism, even a burgeoning anticomputer movement, divisive and seriously inhibiting man's well-being and advancement. Hence the popularity of movements back to simpler times and situations—small towns and open spaces. The crowded, polluted, crushing lives they lead in giant cities are killing the spirits of many good people. These are the fruits of technological advance.

But, a big but, it is the same worrisome technology that is so vitally necessary in all its sophistication to save our surroundings and anything that resembles a decent society. Transportation, pollution control, the continued harvesting of an unyielding, overused planet, await the computer's touch, will die without it. Because, too, the computer is a great engine of reason (unlike man it is essentially incapable of unreason), only a fool would deny its applicability to social, humanistic and philosophical pursuits.

The real world verily shouts to us, however, on this last point. Society is going to apply computer capabilities to our great social problems for the most part only in response to intense political pressures. Indeed, there are too many in government who fear, as political leaders in almost any country must fear, that they would suffer politically if selective knowledge became widely available freely and swiftly by computer. People don't want to drown in facts, but they do want quickly and accurately the information needed to make good and proper decisions. Government must lead in this. Can we elect representatives—and help to guide them through electronic, two-way polling perhaps—representatives who will respond to the feedback from their real bosses? It might not be too much to wish for—a society of caring, stability and happiness.

In Orwell's *1984*, a perverted technology has destroyed freedom, dignity, joy, peace, work and everything good in the old civilization; the childhood rhyme,

> Oranges and lemons
> Say the bells of St. Clements

is a forbidden, stabbing shard from the past. There are those who wonder now whether it can happen here, in the real 1984 or before. We must use our own brainpower first, then our technology and all our resources, to prevent it. And the feared computer is our greatest tool, weapon, protection, good angel and bad. Frank Kelly of the Center for the Study of Democratic Institutions was quoted in the *Los Angeles Times* (March 17, 1973):

> Since Hiroshima, we have known that the "old man" must die. The man of devouring ambition, the consuming man, must give way to the new man, the earning man, the man of understanding,

the servant of life. The future depends upon our opening of ourselves. . . .

There's a power to be grasped before it's lost. There's an endless amount to be learned about what computers can yield—of the evils that can befall us if we fail to master the fear, the mistrust and the hate.

Is it possible that the young sense something adults fail to, that with computerized activity almost totally surrounding it, the majority of the population may find itself intellectually obsolete? Work itself obsolete? Jobs in the sense that we know them become fewer and fewer, and less and less necessary. A life ethic is no less sacred and ancient than a work ethic. It seems strange that we have to repeat and repeat what we really know in our marrow and what man long ago acted upon, or acts upon in civilizations other than ours, that self-esteem is *not* solely dependent on how a person keeps busy, works, holds a job, a position, brings home the bacon, wins his bread. With computers and automation, the great god productivity seems finally in the hands it's supposed to be in, the machines'. Work can for once become more like a game, and games more like work, the means for both measuring and exercising one's gifts. As the necessary work of the world is accomplished, largely by machines, and by those who like to invent them, test them, answer for them, then there'll be no need for the time-serving of listless attendants.

As the machines take over and, in the words of William Emerson, the work ethic "cinders out," there will have to be means of employing the disemployed in something other than wage-paying jobs. The only job left for most might be *to be,* not to get in the way, of oneself and of the others. For a career, young person, get into "human relations"—teaching, sociology, psychiatry, child care, nursing the aged. The hell of such an age may be like that in Jean-Paul Sartre's *No Exit,* where the eternal damnation is the inescapability from other people.

And maybe education and guidance in human relations are not needed. Leisure, when it becomes a way of life, might be better self-taught, not have to be organized or programmed. Regimentation, after all, being a statistic, a unit in a PERT network, a dispensable part of a quota, is what we've had to be taught. Free time and respect for self and others may be the best teachers in the end. Boredom is the recourse and resource of the powerless. With the information everyone needs to find a meaningful place in the world, boredom won't make any sense. Nor will mischief and uproar.

In the meantime, no one has to be reminded, it also makes little sense to start buying shares in Utopia Inc. There are problems enough to deal with: a population, for one, that shows every indication of doubling before the end of the century. Will there be ways to feed these numbers without despoiling the earth and without strangling one national economy more or less in one massive, continuous game of multinational cutthroat? Will we have the good sense to stop the crowding into gigantic cities? one megalopolis paving its way into another, a world of oceans, gleaming asphalt, car dumps, and fast-food pagodas? (We deserve a break . . . someday.)

There'll have to be places to get away to, for true privacy, escape from emotional strain and from the friction with undesirable people and places. Patience, always in short supply, will surely be a necessity, to avoid belligerence and selfishness. With a foreign policy founded on abrasiveness one day and peace-seeking the next, it's not easy to find a place for the common decencies and virtues in everyday life. Can a new society, any more readily than the society of the present, avoid oppressive, inflexible and self-defeating restraints? Can one be at once self-assured and not self-satisfied and intolerant of the maverick, the people who doubt and question, argue, think as individuals, create their own worlds doing no harm? It's tempting to conjure a world "less established" than what we know, turned away from conformity, from forcing the individual to justify his every act if only in his own mind, a world where everyone is not serving only his own self-interest, enlightened or otherwise. To hell with golden rules that work only one way, the way the man in charge, or the elite, says they will.

There might come a world of hundreds of thousands of minorities, people with idiosyncratic loyalties and intelligences, ever curious and questing after their own private visions.

Even computers in such a world could do their best work, be most productive, and not keep information as the preserve of the few. In an elite society, elite throughout, there's no need for team elites, nor for those with a mindless impatience with learning. The hopeless and the despairing might even gain vision, drive and desire from what they see about them. All of this can take place if the machines of information transfer and cybernetic control can create an atmosphere congenial to thinking and reason. So man might be forced to think, for lack of anything worse to do, to stop and think, to think clearly, and to come to a conviction that most "truths" aren't immutable, that work and virtue aren't synonymous, that leisure and fun aren't redundant.

Bibliography

Adams, Henry. *The Education of Henry Adams.* Ernest Samuels, ed. Boston: Houghton Mifflin, 1973.

Adler, Rodney R. *Vertical Transportation for Buildings.* New York: American Elsevier, 1970.

Annual Report 1974. Control Data Corp., 1975.

Annual Report, 1973. Retail Credit Co., 1974.

Annual Report, 1974. Retail Credit Co., 1975.

Arendt, Hannah. *Crises of the Republic.* New York: Harcourt Brace Jovanovich, 1972.

"Astronomy: Photographing a Has-Been." *New York Times,* 6 April 1975, sec. 4, p. 8.

"Automated Payments Concern Canadians." *Computerworld,* 19 March 1975, p. 2.

Bagdikian, Ben H. *The Information Machines: Their Impact on Men and the Media.* New York: Harper & Row, 1971.

Baker, Russell. "The Pornography of Unemployment." *New York Times Magazine,* 20 April 1975, p. 6.

Bartee, Thomas C. *Digital Computer Fundamentals.* 2nd ed. New York: McGraw-Hill, 1966.

Beaumont, Richard A., and Helfgott, Roy B. *Management, Automation and People.* Chicago: Industrial Relations Counselors, 1964.

Bechter, D. M. "The Retirement Decision: Economic Pressures and Economic Trends." *Federal Reserve Bank of Kansas City Monthly Review*, November 1972, pp. 14–23.

Beer, Stafford. "Adaptations in Systems: The Human Approach." In *Rethinking the Practice of Management*. The Diebold Group, ed. New York: Praeger, 1973.

———. "Cybernetic Thrills and Threats." *The Computer Bulletin*, March 1968, reprinted in *Christian Action*, December 1967.

———. "Managing Modern Complexity." *Computers and People*, April 1974.

Bell, Daniel. *The Coming of Post-Industrial Society: A Venture in Social Forecasting*. New York: Basic Books, 1973.

Berkeley, Edmund C. *The Computer Revolution*. New York: Doubleday, 1962.

Biddle, A. G. W. "IBM *vs* AT&T." *On Line Newsletter*, November 1974, pp. 3–7.

Binder, David. "U.S. Believes No New Weaponry Has Fallen to the Communists." *New York Times*, 5 April 1975, p. 9.

Bogart, Dodd H., and Tipps, Havens C. "The Thread from Species O." *The Futurist*, April 1973, pp. 63–65.

Boyd, Jerry. "GAO Tells Congress That Federal DP Spending Is Difficult to Pin Down." *Computer Decisions*, August 1973, p. 6.

Brown, Les. "National TV Planned for 1976." *New York Times*, 15 April 1975, p. 72.

Burge, W. Lee. *The Free Flow of Business Information: Key to Our Credit Economy*. Retail Credit Co., August 1973.

Burnett, Gerald J., and Nolan, Richard. "At Last, Major Roles for Minicomputers." *Harvard Business Review*, May–June 1975.

"By Law the Government Is Disclosing More." *New York Times*, 20 April 1975, sec. 4, p. 7.

"Cal Tech Primitive Robot Sorts Stuff." Santa Ana *Register*, 18 March 1973, p. 6.

Carroll, John B.; Davies, Peter; and Richman, Barry. *The American Heritage Word Frequency Book*. Boston/New York: Houghton Mifflin and American Heritage, 1971.

"Checks Proposed from Passbooks." *New York Times*, 8 April 1975, p. 49.

Chomsky, Noam. *Aspects of the Theory of Syntax*. Cambridge, Mass.: MIT Press, 1965.

———. "Language and the Mind II." *Columbia Forum*, Fall 1966.

Clarke, Arthur C. *2001: A Space Odyssey*. New York: New American Library, 1968.

"A Compromise on Intelligence Data." *New York Times*, 20 April 1975, sec. 4, p. 4.
"A Computerized Look at Medieval Times." *New York Times*, 20 April 1975, sec. 4, p. 4.
"The Computer Goes to Market." *New York Times*, 20 April 1975, sec. 4, p. 4.
"Computers Operating with Ideas." *Computers and People*, March 1975.
Control Program-Five (CP-V). Xerox (El Segundo, Cal.), 1974.
Cote, Alfred J. *The Search for the Robots*. New York: Basic Books, 1967.
Data Security and Data Processing, vol. 1, *Introduction and Overview*. IBM, 1974.
———, vol. 2, *Study Summary*. IBM, 1974.
———, vol. 3, part 1, *State of Illinois: Executive Overview*. IBM, 1974.
———, vol. 3, part 2, *Study Results: State of Illinois*. IBM, 1974.
———, vol. 4, *Study Results: MIT*. IBM, 1974.
———, vol. 5, *Study Results: TRW Systems, Inc.* IBM, 1974.
———, vol. 6, *Evaluations and Installation Experiences: Resource Security System*. IBM, 1974.
Davies, Peter, ed. *The American Heritage School Dictionary*. Boston: Houghton Mifflin and American Heritage, 1972.
Davis, Gordon B. *Introduction to Electronic Computers*. 2nd ed. New York: McGraw-Hill, 1971.
Denahan, Donal. "Computer Love." *New York Times*, 9 April 1975, p. 28.
The Diebold Group, ed. *Rethinking the Practice of Management*. New York: Praeger, 1973.
Drake, Lundell E. "Data Gathering on Dissidents Was 'Out of Control.'" *Computerworld*, 5 December 1973.
Drucker, Peter F. "Information as a Management Resource." In *Rethinking the Practice of Management*. The Diebold Group, ed. New York: Praeger, 1973.
———. *Technology, Management and Society*. Harper & Row, 1973.
Edelson, Harry. *The Office Equipment Industry: Eight Key Questions*. Drexel Burnham, December 1974.
Ellul, Jacques. *Propaganda: The Formation of Men's Attitudes*. New York: Knopf, 1969.
"Federal Crimebusting." *New York Times*, 24 March 1975, p. 30.
Fisher, Harrison. *Today's Business Machines*. Chicago: American Technical Society, 1959.

Flanagan, James L. "The Synthesis of Speech." *Scientific American*, February 1972, pp. 48–56.

———, et al. "Synthetic Voices for Computers." *IEEE Spectrum*, October 1970, pp. 22–45.

Forsythe, Alexandra I. *Computer Science: A Primer*. New York: John Wiley, 1969.

Frank, Howard, and Hopewell, Lynn. "Network Reliability." *Datamation*, August 1974, pp. 85–91.

French, Nancy. "Health Data Banks Feared Sign of Social Control." *Computerworld*, 10 July 1974, p. 4.

Friedmann, Georges. *Le Travail en Miettes*. Paris, France: Gallimard, 1964.

Frisch, Ivan T., and Frank, Howard. *Computer Communications*. Glen Cove, N.Y.: Network Analysis Corp., n. d.

Gabrielli, F. R. "Right of Privacy and Medical Computing." *Datamation*, April 1970, p. 173. Extracted in *Study Results: MIT*, vol. 4, *Data Security and Data Processing*.

Galbraith, John Kenneth. *The New Industrial State*. Boston: Houghton Mifflin, 1967.

Gardner, Howard. *The Quest for Mind: Piaget, Levi-Strauss and the Structuralist Movement*. New York: Knopf, 1973.

Gardner, Martin. *Logic Machines, Diagrams and Boolean Algebra*. New York: Dover, 1958, 1968.

Gielow, Frank C., Jr. *Introducing the Computer*. IBM, 1972.

Golden, Soma. "Economic Models Now Big Business." *New York Times*, 8 April 1975, p. 49.

Goldstine, Herman H. *The Computer: From Pascal to von Neumann*. Princeton, N.J.: Princeton University Press, 1972.

Grand Larousse Encyclopédie. 10 vols. Paris, France: Librairie Larousse, 1960.

Hargraves, Robert F. "The Dartmouth Time-Sharing Network." In *Computer Communications Networks*. Abramson, N., and Kuo, F. F., eds. Englewood Cliffs, N.J.: Prentice-Hall, 1974. Cited in Frisch and Frank.

Heath, Brooks N. "Western Electric's Motivation and Enrichment Trial." *Management Review*, March 1975, pp. 40–43. Condensed from *Industrial Engineering*, November 1974, pp. 14–21.

Heilbroner, Robert L. "None of Your Business." *New York Review of Books*, 20 March 1975, pp. 6–10. A review of books on multinational corporations.

 Honeywell at West Point. Waltham, Mass.: Honeywell, 1974.

Horrock, Nicholas M. "The FBI's Appetite for Very Small Potatoes." *New York Times*, 23 March 1975, sec. 4, p. 2.

———. "I.R.S. Is Now Collecting Much More Than Taxes." *New York Times*, 20 April 1975, sec. 4, p. 4.

———. "A Safe Streets Act But Few Safe Streets." *New York Times*, 13 April 1975, sec. 4, p. 5.

"How Many Jobless . . . How Many Jobs." *New York Times*, 23 April 1975, p. 42.

IBM. *The Computer Comes of Age.* IBM, n. d.

———. *Computers Are Going to Town.* IBM, 1972.

———. *Data Processing Glossary.* 5th ed. IBM, 1972.

———. *Introduction to IBM Processing Systems: Student Text.* 4th ed. IBM, 1970.

———. *Learning and the Computer.* IBM, n. d.

———. *Problem Solving by Linear Programming.* IBM, n. d.

———. *Programming as a Career.* IBM, n. d.

———. *Programming: Words that Move Machines.* IBM, 1973.

———. *The Science in Management Science.* IBM, n. d.

———. *Simulation: Modeling Reality.* IBM, 1973.

IBM Research Highlights, Feburary 1975.

"If the Machine Wants Our Jobs, Let's Buy It." *Life*, 14 August 1964. A report on the conference of the Ad Hoc Committee on the Triple Revolution (weaponry, automation, human rights); included in the report, Gunnar Myrdal, Linus Pauling, Michael Heilbroner, Tom Hayden, Todd Gitlin, Robert Theobald, Roy Harrod; the report submitted to President Lyndon B. Johnson.

Johnson, Ronald. "A Look at People as Machines." *Media and Methods*, February 1974, pp. 53–61. A review of Lewis Yablonsky, *Robopaths: People as Machines*, New York: Penguin.

Jones, Stacy V. "Information System Introduced." *New York Times*, 5 April 1975, p. 37.

Kilborn, Peter T. "IBM's Earnings Advance Only 1.4%." *New York Times*, 11 April 1975, p. 45.

———. "White-Collar Unemployment: No End in Sight." *New York Times*, 23 February 1975, sec. 3, p. 1.

King, Paul A. "Personnel Trends '73: Will the Executive Go AWOL?" *Administrative Management*, January 1973, p. 20.

Kleinschmidt, Walter A. "Some Predictions to Start a New Year." *Administrative Management*, January 1973, p. 17.

Kochenburger, Ralph J., and Turcio, Carolyn J. *Computers in Modern Society.* Santa Barbara: Hamilton, 1974.

Kohlmeier, Louis M. "Computer Work Isn't Patentable . . ." *Wall Street Journal*, 21 November 1972.

Kučera, Henry. "Computers in Language Analysis and in Lexicography." In *The American Heritage Dictionary of the English Language.* William Morris, ed.

Laing, R. D. *The Divided Self.* New York: Pantheon, 1969.

Leonard, George. "In God's Image." *Saturday Review*, 22 February 1975, pp. 12–14.

Levenstein, Aaron. "Work—What Is the Future?" *Freedom at Issue*, July–August 1974, pp. 5–10.

Lewis, Flora. "Labor Relations in Europe." *New York Times*, 25 March 1975, p. 1.

Lindsey, Robert. "Consumers Test Electronic Banking." *New York Times*, 6 April 1975, sec. 3, p. 1.

———. "Some Who Believe in a No-Work Ethic." *New York Times*, 1 June 1975, p. 45.

Littell, Richard. "Sweden Enacts Program to Make Workers . . . Safe and Happy." *New York Times*, 13 February 1975, p. 45.

McCarthy, E. J., et al., *Integrated Data Processing Systems.* New York: John Wiley, 1966.

McElheny, Victor K. "Electronics Brings a Quiet Revolution in Phoning Service." *New York Times*, 6 April 1975, p. 1.

McLuhan, Marshall. *Understanding Media.* 2nd ed. New York: New American Library, 1964.

———; Fiore, Quentin; and Agel, Jerome. *War and Peace in the Global Village.* New York: Bantam, 1968.

McMillan, Brockway. "Theory and Principles: The Intellectual Framework." *Bell Laboratories Record*, January 1975, pp. 83–89.

McRae, Norman A. *The Economist*, January 1972.

Madden, Richard L. "President's Mail Is Sifted for Sampling of Trends." *New York Times*, 31 March 1975, p. 10.

Marcuse, Herbert. *Reason and Revolution: Hegel and the Rise of Social Theory.* 2nd ed., with supplementary chapter. New York: Humanities Press, 1954.

Martin, James, and Norman, Adrian R. D. *The Computerized Society.* Englewood Cliffs, N.J.: Prentice-Hall, 1970.

May, Rollo. *Power and Innocence: A Search for the Sources of Violence.* New York: Norton, 1972.

Morris, William, ed. *The American Heritage Dictionary of the English Language.* Boston/New York: Houghton Mifflin and American Heritage, 1969.

Neier, Aryeh. *Dossier: The Secret Files* They *Keep on* You. New York: Stein and Day, 1975.

Nestle, Elliot. "Design Workshop: Configuring an Actual Data System." In *Electronic Deskbook: Data Communications Systems.* New York: McGraw-Hill, 1972.

The New York Times Information Bank. The New York Times Co., 1972.

Nordsieck, H. "The Metaconta Switching System." *Electrical Communications,* vol. 46, no. 4, 1971.

Orwell, George. *1984.* Afterword by Erich Fromm. New York: New American Library, 1961.

Ottinger, Richard L. "MaBellOpoly." *New York Times,* 19 April 1975, p. 31.

Parker, Donn B.; Nycum, Susan; and Oüra, S. Stephen. *Computer Abuse.* Palo Alto, Cal.: Stanford Research Institute, 1973.

Pfeffer, Richard M. "The Worker as Commodity: When the Niceties Go." *New York Times,* 30 April 1975, p. 41.

"Postal Surveillance Placed over 8,500 over Last Two Years." *New York Times,* 19 March 1975, p. 28.

Potts, George W. *Minicomputer Industry: Riding the Tide of Technology.* New York: Dean Witter, 1974.

Quine, W. V. *Selected Logic Papers.* New York: Random House, 1966.

Raskin, A. H. "Jobs for the Jobless." *New York Times,* 18 March 1975, p. 37.

Reich, Charles A. *Greening of America.* New York: Random House, 1970.

Reif, Rita. " 'Word Processing' Comes of Age." *New York Times,* 4 May 1975, sec. 3, p. 5.

Rensberger, Boyce. "Genetic Mutation Called Minor Evolutionary Factor." *New York Times,* 18 April 1975, p. 31.

———. "Man and Computer: Uneasy Allies of 25 Years." *New York Times,* 27 June 1972, p. 27.

Rogers, Thomas. "Astro's Watson Scores Millionth Run." *New York Times,* 5 May 1975, p. 47.

Rosenberg, Jerry M. *The Death of Privacy.* New York: Random House, 1969.

Russell, David P. *The IDR System.* Reuters, 1975.

Saffian, Steven R. "DIAL, a New Campus Information Access System." *NASPA Journal,* October 1973.

Sagan, Carl. "In Praise of Robots." *Computers and People,* May 1975, pp. 8–12.

Sanford, Phil. "The Automated Battlefield." *New York Times Magazine*, 23 February 1975, pp. 12ff.

Schlafly, Hubert J. *The Computer in the Living Room.* Teleprompter, 1973.

Sippl, Charles J. *Computer Dictionary.* Indianapolis: Howard W. Sams, 1966.

———, and Sippl, Charles P. *Computer Dictionary.* Indianapolis: Howard W. Sams, 1974.

Skinner, B. F. *Beyond Freedom and Dignity.* New York: Knopf, 1971.

Slotnick, D. L. "The Fastest Computer." *Scientific American*, February 1971, pp. 76–87.

Smith, Gene. "Electronic Device Said to Cut Use of 'Gas' and Other Fuels." *New York Times*, 21 March 1975, p. 1.

Snow, C. P. "Science and the Advanced Society." *Computers and Automation*, April 1966, pp. 14–17.

Soble, Ronald L., and Dallos, Robert E. *The Impossible Dream; The Equity Funding Story: The Fraud of the Century.* New York: G. P. Putnam's Sons, 1975.

Sontag, Susan. Reply to the Editor on "The Meaning of Vietnam." *New York Review of Books*, 12 June 1975, p. 24.

Sterzer, Fred. "An Electronic License Plate for Motor Vehicles." *RCA Review*, June 1974.

Stevens, Leonard A. *Explorers of the Brain.* New York: Knopf, 1971.

Stevens, William K. "Auto Workers at Lordstown . . ." *New York Times*, 19 March 1975, p. 28.

Stewart, John. "Science: Political and Personal." *Science for People*, September 1974, pp. 6–7.

Strayer, Joseph R., and Munro, Dana C. *The Middle Ages: 395–1500.* New York: Appleton, Century, Crofts, 1959.

"The Swedish Data Act." *Current Sweden*, #4, July 1973.

Sweet, William B. "Addressing Technique Unlocks Minicomputer's Extended Memory." *Electronics*, 8 November 1973.

"Time Inc. Unit to Use Satellites . . ." *Wall Street Journal*, 11 April 1975, p. 21.

Time for Innovation: Honeywell at the University of Waterloo. Waltham, Mass.: Honeywell, 1974.

Toffler, Alvin. *The Eco-Spasm Report.* New York: Bantam, 1975.

———. *Future Shock.* New York: Bantam, 1971.

TRW Inc. Form 10-K, 1974, to Securities and Exchange Commission.

Turn, Rein. *Computers in the 1980s.* New York: Columbia University Press, 1974.

United States of America *vs* International Business Machines, 69 Civ. 200/72-344 (D. N. E.), *Pretrial Brief for Defendant,* 15 January 1975.

Vinge, P. G. *Swedish Data Act.* #43. Federation of Swedish Industries, 1973.

Ways, Max. "Business Faces Growing Pressure to Behave Better." *Fortune,* May 1974.

Weaver, Warren, Jr. "High Court Denies Computer Patent for Programming." *New York Times,* 21 November 1972.

What Is a Credit Bureau? Associated Credit Bureaus, Inc., 1974.

White, John W. "The Consciousness Revolution." *Saturday Review,* 22 February 1975, pp. 15–19.

Whiteman, T. Mary. "Computer Elicits Mixed Feelings in Canadian Study." *Computerworld,* 5 December 1973, p. 3.

Whiteside, Thomas. "Anything Adverse." *The New Yorker,* 21 April 1975, pp. 45–101.

Wilson, Ira G. and Marthann E. *What Computers Cannot Do.* New York: Auerbach, 1970.

Wilson, Robert A. "Group Technology Set for U.S. Invasion." *Iron Age,* 24 February 1975, pp. 35–37.

Winckelmann, W. A. "Automatic Intercept System." *Bell Laboratories Record,* May 1968, pp. 139–43.

Winograd, Terrence. "When Will Computers Understand People?" *Psychology Today,* May 1974, pp. 74–77.

Witkin, Richard. "Computerized Chrysler Engine . . ." *New York Times,* 11 April 1975, p. 1.

"Word Processing." *Government Executive,* January 1974.

The Xerox 550 Computer. Xerox (El Segundo, Cal.), 1974.

The Xerox 560 Computer. Xerox (El Segundo, Cal.), 1974.

Xerox Control Program for Real Time. Xerox (El Segundo, Cal.), 1974.

Index